HER BATTLE

MY LESSONS

OUR JOURNEY

A Husband's Account
Up Close ♀ Very Personal

SHAWN C. MACKEY, SR.

Copyright

HER BATTLE, MY LESSONS, OUR JOURNEY

Copyright © 2022 Shawn C. Mackey

For permission, contact the author at:

drshawncmackey@gmail.com

www.shawncmackey.com

ISBN: 978-1-64775-588-1

Warning:
This book contains graphic images of a sensitive and mature nature.

Imagine A World Without Cancer
By Michele Rosa

Imagine there's no cancer.
It's easy if you try.
No pain or suffering
Or waiting just to die.

Imagine all the people
Living worry free,
Without that ticking time bomb
That no one else can see.

You may say I'm a dreamer,
But I'm not the only one
That hopes the world will be cancer-free
So, we can live as one.

DEDICATION

I would like to dedicate this book to my mom, Rose Mary Mackey-Thompson, my wife, Dr. Teresa L. Mackey, and our children, Christopher, Shawn, and Matthew.

In memory of my mom, who was always full of life, compliments and criticisms, joy, love, and laughter. She unselfishly opened her heart and home to family, community, and strangers alike. Because of her, I am able to glide along on her heavenly wings, pursuing a future that she would be proud of. I pray that it is so.

It is with gratitude and unfailing love that I dedicate this book to my wife. Life created a fire for her to endure, and she used the heat as fuel to triumph. In truth, this is my story but her battle. I am honored and humbled to share this journey with her. Forever and ever. I pray that it is so.

To our wonderful boys, I hope that time reveals the pride inherent in this dedication. They are young men growing into their own. I rejoice in being the best father I can be to them, realizing there is no greater responsibility or gift. They were taught character and integrity when all else seemed out of reach. These core principles will guide their lives and foster greatness within them. I pray that it is so.

ACKNOWLEDGMENTS

When the idea captured my imagination and I began writing this book, I initially did not consult with my wife. This was different because we collaborate on all things *us*. I avoided the conversation initially because I knew how sensitive, revealing, and possibly even embarrassing this book could be. It is extremely transparent. The book reveals my perspective of our battle with cancer; however, it is truly her breast cancer journey at the core. In short, without her experiences and support, this book would not exist.

Despite exposing some of my wife's and our family's most difficult and personal vulnerabilities, my wife agreed the book could serve a greater purpose. She believes that she could empower, strengthen, and encourage others who are forced to walk the same path through her pain, powerlessness, and hardships.

I must acknowledge her sacrifice and willingness to offer her story to benefit so many others. I know her desire would be for this book to reach beyond our circle in hopes of magnifying the message while highlighting her struggle, growth, accomplishments, sacrifices, and ultimately, her victory. In short, I am eternally grateful for her trust in this project and the love she has shown to allow me to share her battle.

CONTENTS

Life is like a box of chocolates; you never know what you're going to get. ~ Forrest Gump

FOREWORDS

I really enjoyed reading this book. It bought back some special memories for me during my family's journey and victory. It had some very funny stories to temper the serious subject matter. I believe this book will definitely help some husbands understand the process of being a true partner during this most difficult time. Well Done!!!

Dexter Holloway

Having closely watched two loved ones battle cancer (one sadly succumbed), I debated my feelings on the title and even questioned Shawn on the book itself-until I read it. It's timely, extremely palatable, and relatable to any one of the human race that's experienced a traumatic family ordeal. As a woman, I appreciate how Shawn takes great care to buffer his lovely wife's exposure, while he himself is wholly transparent and vulnerable about his lessons learned. It is a much-needed refreshing view from the other side of the bed. The lens of any husband or partner just became a lot clearer because Shawn illuminated a narrow, dimly-lit path and made it more navigable. "Her Battle, His Lessons, Our Journey" is intimate and a riveting, universal blueprint that allows for the continuance of a beautiful journey through controversy and triumph.

LTC (Ret) Cadetta Bridges-Breaker

It has been my great fortune in life to call Shawn and Teresa Mackey colleagues and friends. The first time I met Shawn, when he was a young professional just starting out in his career, I was struck by his intellect, his kindness, his wit, and his devotion to his family. He brings all of that to bear in this book and more. Through his writing, Shawn walks you through what it is like to confront one of the most difficult challenges a couple can face – a triple-negative breast cancer diagnosis. Make no mistake, this may be an instructional book about helping a spouse navigate cancer, but it is much more than that. It is a real-life love story, told with brutal honesty, self-effacing humor, and grace.

Debra West, Ph.D.

Dear Reader,

This is the first foreword that I have ever written or even been asked to write. I was so honored when Shawn asked me to write this foreword to his book, and I was so surprised to find out that Shawn had written a book. You see, I've known Shawn for more than twenty-four years. We met when we both worked for a non-profit in Memphis, Chickasaw Council, Boy Scouts of America. We became fast friends, and I immediately knew that Shawn was one of the smartest people I've ever met. He was so passionate about his work, education, family, and friends. I was always amazed when he spoke. People listened because it was thoughtful, it was straightforward, and it was the truth.

Early in our friendship, I knew Shawn's goals of education and his desire to be an administrator in the Community College system. He once told me when we were in graduate school at Delta State University that he wanted to be President of a Community College. I knew he would do what it took to achieve this goal. Like I said, he is passionate about education and his work. He is also passionate about his family and friends. He has always strived to be a great father, son, brother, and friend. Then one day, Shawn told me about Teresa and their great love. I knew that she was very special because Shawn didn't give his heart to just anyone.

Yes, I have known Shawn for a long time. I have looked to him through the years for advice and friendship. However, what I didn't know was that one day, Shawn would go through this very personal journey and would write a book about such a private moment in time for his family. But his desire to write this book will help so many people with their own personal struggles and journey.

This book, *Her Battle, My Lessons, and Our Journey*, is powerful, inspirational, and a true love story. Shawn took the passion that I have admired about him through the years, and wrote a beautiful, real-life love story about a personal journey that he and his wife, Teresa, along with their boys, went through after Teresa was diagnosed with breast cancer. The story is real and raw, and very personal. It is a powerful journey told through a husband's perspective as they navigate through the surgery, treatment, and support that Teresa needed as she battled cancer.

This book has changed my life for the better. It has given me a perspective that I didn't have or even know that I needed. For that, I am eternally grateful. Through the years, we have shared a lot of stories, laughter, and memories. But mostly, we have shared a friendship that I will treasure forever.

Emily Ratliff Havens, Executive Director of GRAMMY
Museum Mississippi but most importantly, a Friend

11

"The human spirit is stronger than anything that can happen to it." ~C.C. Scott

PREFACE

I really did not want to be here, if I'm being honest. I do not mean alive. I mean, right here at this moment, revealing so much. Yet, despite my reservations, fears, and vulnerabilities, I am compelled to share her battle, my story, and our journey. My hope is that this book will generate more dialogue and support for a subject that I believe needs much more attention. You see, we cannot always control the events of our lives, but we can decide how we respond and process our emotions to those events. Each of us must consider what we can learn from this experience. What are the principles and the purpose beyond the pain or tragedy of the moment?

In this book, I will be discussing highly sensitive details about my wife's cancer battle and my intimate role as husband, caretaker, and champion. I refer to it as *our* journey because it was – it is. While I did not physically carry cancer in my body, as her husband, I carried it emotionally and spiritually, which absolutely affected me mentally and physically. To say that I was unprepared is a grave understatement. At times my perspective may seem selfish or insensitive, but this is how I felt in those moments. While I am apprehensive regarding your judgment, that apprehensiveness is outweighed by my desire to be transparent as I hope to help someone who may be on the same journey. Here's the truth: you cannot effectively process things, good or bad, if you don't acknowledge and confront them. It is important to point out that in order for me to write the details of what I have experienced, my wife had to be okay with it. This is my truth, but it was and still is her cross to bear. In a sense, I'm exposing one of the darkest moments in her life as I fight to discover my own path's light.

As I wrote, I often found myself including little *disclaimers* or *apologies* when describing unpleasant moments because I was concerned about how it made me look to even have the thoughts and reactions I had. But the truth is, you cannot plan for this invader/disease or the emotions and feelings you have - whether you've been married for six months, one year, or twenty years. You have to accept its existence, then attack it Independence Day style, as if you're Will Smith or Jeff Goldblum. So let's go!

Challenges are what make life interesting overcoming them is what makes life meaningful.

~Joshua Marine

INTRODUCTION

What am I supposed to do? How am I supposed to act? What should I say and how do I say it? What can I expect of her behavior, attitude, emotional stability, and physical appearance? I had these and many other questions engulfing my thoughts and sanity when we were hit with the reality of a breast cancer diagnosis. Initially, I turned to the omnipotent, the source of all sources, the answer to all problems, the ultimate truth teller– Google. I turned to Google to answer many of the questions I had confounding me. While Google had a lot of articles and books on breast cancer, there were few that explained to me how to feel. Thankfully, I remembered a very close friend who mentioned to me in a previous conversation that his wife was a breast cancer survivor. One day while golfing together, I confided in him, and he gave me some advice that I never forgot. It went like this, and I quote: "Just shut the hell up and don't say anything; just listen because not sh*t you say will be right." I knew there had to be someone else that I could talk to that would reveal a better pathway forward for me. A safer, more engaging, comforting, and loving path that did not involve suffering in silence.

I knew that I did not have an appetite for speaking with a professional counselor, regardless of their training and background. While that may seem counterproductive, in my mind, if the person I was talking to had never experienced the devastation of cancer in their home, they would be limited in scope, understanding, and ability to provide positive guidance to me. Most importantly, I questioned if a counselor or therapist could help me understand how to create a safe, loving space for my wife and me to attack, endure, adopt and adapt to a newness that would define us throughout our cancer battle. I cannot emphasize how important I believed life experiences mattered for one to function in this space properly. No cancer experience meant no basis to explore my fragile emotional state. Additionally,

I was adamant that a *female* counselor could not advise me on how to engage unless her situation replicated mine in some capacity. I also was cautious about a white counselor. After all, I am married to an intelligent, successful, independent black woman who is filled with black culture. The cultural differences could potentially complicate things further. In my opinion, there is no creature on this earth like the black woman. Could a white male counselor identify with my experience as a black man whose wife had cancer? I was soon forced to put aside all of my individuality as a black man on this journey. I quickly learned that color, race, creed, and gender be damned. This was *all of our* fight. The cancer strategy may be vastly different, but the battle is the same, and the goal is the same: TO SURVIVE!

I didn't need to make any distinctions based on race or gender, or age because cancer certainly didn't. The data shows that cancer is one of the most equal-opportunity killers that exists in America today. It attacks the poor with the same vengeance as the wealthy. It devastates black households at the same rate as white households or other demographics. Cancer destroys young boys and girls with the same tenacity as adult men and women. Frankly, it is a well-known, unshakable, constant, and tenacious killer with a ferocious appetite. It does not discriminate. It is not courteous or politically correct. It's a surprise gut punch right before the finish line of a marathon after training for it for years. It rattles your plans. It makes you question your faith. It disrupts your family, and it has no regard for your tears or your fears. Make no mistake, cancer is a non-discriminatory enemy.

This book is written with a few goals in mind: First, I hope that it is a resource for other men (black, white, and other) like me that need to understand the predicament of supporting a wife fighting the deadly and vicious intruder that is *cancer*. Resources for spouses dealing with any level of sickness that requires them to operate as primary support or caregivers should be much more plentiful and publicized. I'm not saying there are none. But I am saying I didn't have a clue where to start or who to ask, which definitely caused more anxiety during an already stressful time.

Secondly, I hope the book serves as a tool kit for learning - not so much about the disease because there is plenty of literature out there about that - but about the emotional toll and mental stability that you must possess to survive. I will not exhaust the point here that women and men are different; that's obvious. There have been many books and articles already written on this subject. The reality, however, is that we do process differently. In situations like these, both perspectives must be considered and heard in a safe, nonjudgmental space for solidarity as a unit.

Thirdly, I hope this book can help prepare a spouse or significant other to deal with the ongoing post-cancer battle, which will challenge the existence, sustainability, and dare I say, survival of the relationship or marriage. Hopefully, this book will help you understand that you are now involved in a new relationship or marriage, which will drastically change.

Additionally, I hope that this book can serve as therapy of sorts for others as writing it did for me. It forced me to identify new barriers and opportunities. Writing this book helped me become a better me because it allowed me to engage in a self-reflection and self-evaluation that gave me the strength to face life's greatest obstacles and made me sensitive enough to see these barriers as opportunities to grow and help others.

Finally, I wanted to honor my wife for the strength and tenacity she demonstrated during this fight. There is no way that the goals I have outlined can be accomplished without truthfully confronting and exploring what you are feeling and being transparent about it. Strap in. Are you ready?

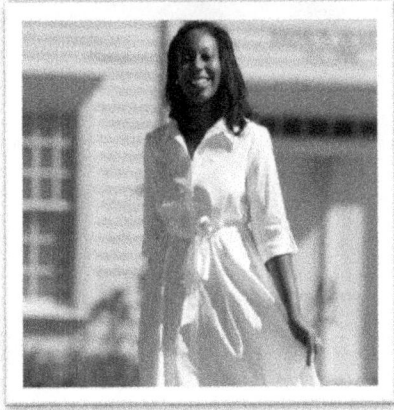

There is only one kind of shock worse than the totally unexpected: the expected for which one has refused to prepare. ~Mary Renault, The Charioteer

Chapter 1

THE DISCOVERY
Prepare for the Worse, Hope for the Best

For the last several years, my wife has typically had abnormal mammograms. According to research, if breast imaging reveals an irregular area of the breast that can be malignant, it is considered an abnormal mammogram. About 10 percent of women who get mammograms experience abnormal ones. Recent research also says that most of the time, additional tests result in no cancer, with fewer than one in ten being cancer. My wife's mammograms revealed a cyst that doctors stated was benign but should always be monitored during her annual breast exam. Therefore, a cyst, mass, or lump was not necessarily uncommon to us. The cyst had to be monitored, but we always had a sense of peace because it was very small, barely detectable, and according to the doctors, noncancerous.

In my role as husband and chief breast examiner, I was happy to do my part in "monitoring" her breast. I would frequently feel her breasts – just doing my part for early detection, but let's just say I was not always focused on the task at hand. You know what I'm saying. I'm not a doctor, but I could play one with just the right amount of encouragement. That's a joke guys. It was funny in my head. Pray for me.

One morning while showering, my wife performed her routine self-breast exam and noticed a small lump, cyst, or mass that seemed more noticeable or pronounced than usual. Still, it was no reason to be alarmed, but all your instincts, suspicions, and years of doctors' counseling mandate that you go and have a mammogram – just to be sure. In my mind, I truly believed that my wife was being a bit paranoid and would remain completely healthy. I figured she would just get another note from the doctor saying that they would keep an eye on it, you know, like in times past. Unfortunately,

I did not attend this doctor's visit. This was not out of the ordinary because I chalked it up to routine. Let me say, in hindsight, I regretted not going because it would ultimately be the day that would ignite a chain of life-altering behaviors and events towards attitudes, love, perseverance, communication, supporters, and health. Honestly, everything changed in the blink of an eye.

The mammogram confirmed my wife's suspicions. Damn it. The mammogram identified a cyst, mass, or lump. I refer to it as a cyst, a lump, or a mass because, depending on the audience, professional or casual, many refer to it by a different name. Again, in my mind, I am still not overly concerned, but now she has my full attention. At this juncture, she is scheduled to have a biopsy to determine if the cyst is cancerous. The cyst was located in the upper right quadrant of her right breast. This part gets a little fuzzy for me; however, I am absolutely certain that my wife can regurgitate every detail. She keeps a journal of everything. I know she has one journal specifically dedicated to chronicling her entire cancer journey. She does not guard the journal with any fervor. In fact, she lays it around quite casually. The same is true for her personal journal. Why am I sharing this inconsequential fact? Surprisingly for three very notable reasons: first, my wife, at this time, does not know that I am writing

> **A NOTE**
> "Men carry the disease with their spouse and need _support_ to be a support."

this book. I wanted it to be raw, authentic, in my own words, and reveal my thoughts, feelings, and reactions. I earnestly want men to understand the significance of every aspect of the process while using my experience to adapt and positively alter their behavior so that they can be their very best selves while enduring this high-stakes journey.

Secondly, I also want the women who read this book to recognize the insecurities and unknowns that men are battling while daring to be supportive, loving, being everything, or for some, nothing at all. In other words, trying to be whatever that moment calls for. Women must recognize that men carry the disease and burden along with them, have unstable feelings, and desire acknowledgment through the suffering.

The final reason is that I genuinely want to respect my wife's privacy. I feel that the journal has been a source of strength for her. I believe her writing provided clarity on cloudy days and inspiration when her kick was not as high. That's a Southern analogy when asked how one is doing. The response might be, "I'm kicking, just not too high." I recognize the journals were her escape, a place where she could cry on the pages and begin anew with each daily writing assignment. I know she needed this outlet of truth desperately. Most importantly, but also less importantly, I wanted her to be able to write my name in private, to elaborate proudly when I exceeded her expectations, or curse my name when I was falling short. The journaling absolutely must be authentic, private, and a small part of therapy that she would own all to herself. It was important to me for her journals to belong to her alone to chronicle her thoughts, feelings, and frustrations.

All of this to say, I could have looked in her journals and had access to every valuable detail (even the meaningless banter), every date; every doctor's name, likes and dislikes, every medication and side effects; treatments; and every type of chemo. In other words, I could have had access to all the details, big and small, to write this book. However, I chose to forgo access to the most comprehensive resource in an attempt to share *my* perspective.

Love bears all things, believes all things,
hopes all things, endures all things.
1 Corinthians 13:7

Chapter 2

NEWLYWEDS
We New to This

Let me pause and point out what I think is a very significant detail. When we found out my wife had cancer, we were newlyweds; and I would argue, we're still newlyweds with only three years under our belt. While we dated a number of years before becoming husband and wife, somehow, circumstances changed after matrimony. We dated secretly for years because we both worked in higher education, specifically community college. There was no conflict of interest, violation of ethics, or unprofessionalism. Still, because we were both senior administrators, we simply did not want others to limit our growth professionally or be the subject of water-cooler banter. We valued our privacy, and it allowed us to adopt an "us against the world" mantra early on. Interesting side note, the primary reason we kept our relationship private would become a self-fulfilling prophecy. In short, very uninformed and ignorant people would use our marriage as a rationale to deny both of us professional growth opportunities. While the professional hiccup is so not the focus of this book, it did a few things for our marriage early on that helped us in our battle with cancer. First, it made us realize that we are *stronger together*. Secondly, we realized regardless of the challenge, with proper planning and preparation, we could survive any obstacle. Lastly, it taught us the value of private and honest communication (still growing in this area). People and circumstances have always challenged our love, but we survive and thrive.

So again, we were not even married a year, but we were preparing to embark upon one of life's most critical battles together. What a monumental challenge of our commitment, love, and support. It gives a real perspective to "till death do us part." It would test our marriage early on to determine if we were built for this. Did we have enough invested in our marriage, specifically each other, to rise to the challenge? Would we, mainly me, look for a pathway out to avoid the stress, trauma, and sacrifice? No hesitation on my part; I was all in. I became a champion for my wife's survival. I knew our love could and would endure. I knew it was stronger than strong. I felt it, I believed it, and most importantly, I desired it. Still, challenges did arise, as you will discern.

I remember saying to myself, "Buckle up, it's about to get real." That was my pep talk as if I were getting game ready with my game face on. I am a positive person but also a realist. I try to remain optimistic, but life has shown that it has the ability to deal blow after blow after continuous blow. So, while I took personal inventory of the man I knew myself to be, I knew more would be demanded of me. My mind, heart, or a combination of the two, would not allow me to waiver in my commitment to seeing this through. Even worse, I could not deny the reality that I, too, could be in the middle of the storm at a moment's notice. My moral compass kept saying it could be her today and me tomorrow. So, I never wavered in my loyalty, love, and commitment to my wife. Literally and figuratively, this would be a story of triumph that our kids and grandkids would read and learn about through the years. That alone gave me the strength to forge forward.

"We must accept finite disappointment, but never lose infinite hope." ~Martin Luther King Jr.

Chapter 3

SO SMALL BUT SO BIG
Little Things Really Do Matter

From the beginning, we both set out to perform a bit of due diligence. It was time to select an oncologist to be our medical partner in this journey. This was an important step because health care is so focused on profit. Doctors form their own networks and pass patients from doctor to doctor in the name of a medical referral. I think we would all agree that a network or doctor recommendation may not always represent the best doctors in the profession, the most well-trained, the one that exhibits excellent bedside manner, or the one that provides the level of access and comfort needed to give adequate reassurance through the process. A referral may contribute to a doctor's bottom line, and sometimes, a particular doctor simply might not be the right fit.

After seeking referrals and conducting our own research, we landed on Dr. Phillip Ley, Surgical Oncologist. Dr. Ley came highly recommended. We were told that he was thorough, kind, straightforward, knowledgeable, and always accessible. And he was. What I appreciated most was his bluntness and directness. He did not offer false pretense or false hope, nor did he tell us what we wanted to hear or provide irresponsible words of comfort. Dr. Ley provided the facts, a prognosis, and a feasible plan to move forward. I think we both respected that approach. Yet, what I most valued was his accessibility and availability. I know my wife texted and called him on weekends, after hours, and on holidays. He responded every single time. It was amazing how he availed himself to us, constantly answering our questions, easing our fears with relevant information, and genuinely representing himself as a partner vested in our journey, survival, and success. We were so grateful and in awe.

The day would arrive for our appointment to visit Dr. Ley to have the cyst biopsied. He gave my wife a little something-something for the pain, which according to her, was not sufficient, and then began the process of inserting a probe into her right breast. I watched in amazement and with a bit of confusion as he aggressively poked and prodded at the cyst. In my mind, I'm thinking, "You are about to aggravate the cyst or cause it to spread!" I envisioned the cancer as a water balloon and figured that the water would ooze out and spread everywhere if you punctured it. I feared the same would occur with the cyst while watching him. The aggression seemed too much for what we thought was a pretty painless and routine procedure. Unfortunately, he had to stick and prod the cyst multiple times because, as he stated, the equipment was old, and he could not locate the cyst properly. My wife and I made eye contact; you know how you look discreetly, hoping no one gets wind of your nonverbal communication. We both looked dissatisfied and now questioned if we had made the best decision for our oncologist. The doubt was short-lived. Dr. Ley finally completed the biopsy, and we were on our way.

A NOTE

"Do your research on your doctors. Get to know them. Be sure that they're a good fit for your battle squad. It matters!"

We had such confidence in Dr. Ley that we were more than willing to accept his referral recommendations. As a result, we were blessed with the care and medical expertise of two outstanding doctors, Dr. Tammy Young, a Medical Oncologist, and Dr. Kenneth Barraza, a Certified Plastic and Reconstructive Surgeon. Both were exceptional.

Dr. Young was very direct with a much more sensitive bedside manner. She was very knowledgeable, informative, and treated my wife with dignity and compassion. Many of the nurses asked my wife who would be performing her breast reconstruction. She, on multiple occasions, answered, "Dr. Barraza." Before either could tell us about his professional representation, they all (and I mean all) stated how handsome he is. Hell, when I met him, I laughingly told my wife they were right. Our affinity for him only increased when I learned he loved golf, was a diehard Saints fan, and a pilot. What a trifecta. See, you get to know the doctors because cancer is not an outpatient experience. You spend a lot of time with the doctors, developing some sense of a professional relationship with them, albeit personal for you. Let me restate that the great ones make you believe you are at the very least a close acquaintance. I am sure all their patients would echo the same sentiments. The trifecta aside, Dr. Barraza knows his way around the breast. Sorry. I mean, he is a brilliant doctor whose work is exceptional and whose work

I get to admire every day — definitely a pair of gifted hands.

The completion of the biopsy procedure and our departure set the clock in motion. Now we had to wait. My vocabulary nor my ability to write can adequately describe the intense emotion of waiting to learn my wife's fate, *our fate*. The cyst, only 1.7 centimeters, about the size of a nickel, appeared so small, but the ramifications would be very substantial. On the way home, we were mostly silent except for a few questions I asked to lighten the mood. Me: "Would you like to get something to eat?" Her: "No, I don't have an appetite." Me: "Me either. What would you like to do?" Her: "Nothing but go home." Me: "Me too."

We were sitting on the sofa watching television when we received a call from Dr. Ley. It was late in the evening on December 27, 2019, I think, around 6 p.m. If I didn't know any better, I would swear that the doctors call after normal business hours, hoping you are in the comfort of your home to receive the call and process the biopsy test results. The reaction at home may be vastly different if in public, or maybe the reaction would be the same. Who knows? We listened on the speaker-phone as he confirmed that my wife had Triple Negative Breast Cancer. He went on to explain that Triple Negative is the most difficult breast cancer to treat and has the highest rate of reoccurrence because of its ability to spread to other parts of the body. He provided other reasons, but they appeared to fade like a sound growing distant in the movies. I'm like W.T.F. So, not only do we have breast cancer, but we also drew the joker out of the deck. If we forced ourselves to look at the glass half-full or acknowledge a bit of good fortune, we also learned that the cancer was in Stage 2. In other words, the cancer had not reached Stage 3 or 4. However, Stage 2 presented the potential for advanced spread from a very advanced cancer stage. The cancer could have also spread to the lymph nodes. So, yes, it was a stretch to acknowledge the smidgen of positive in the big pile of horse sh*t. Husbands or significant others, this was my first real test as we received this news because my reaction would serve as a catalyst for future reactions. It may very well be your first test as well. Not sure why or how, but I thought I had mentally prepared my reaction and response for good or bad news. I was prepared, well, as best I could be.

Dr. Ley went on to outline our treatment plan. His approach mandated that we receive treatment first in an attempt to shrink, dissolve and destroy the cyst, which he recommended begin immediately, followed by surgery. From our research, we knew that most doctors' methods endorsed surgery first to remove the cyst with treatment to follow. Not Dr. Ley. He wanted to see how her body and the cyst would respond to the treatment. Even more important, the treatment would inform us of the complexity of the surgery.

The news was devastating. It ignited a tsunami of tears from both of us. Our bodies were numb, minds scattered, and emotions shot to hell. The shock never goes away. After all, how could

> **A NOTE**
> *"Her courage gave me the strength to fight harder."*

it, seeing how we had drawn the worst card in the breast cancer deck? Triple-Negative. However, as I stated earlier, I was kind of prepared. I knew our reactions could not persist. I allowed my wife to grieve awhile longer as I began to muster up the courage to be her rock. Guys, in case you have not discovered it by now, at this point, the clock has started, and you are completely invested in the battle and journey, and everything you say and do from this point has consequences. Take that to the bank.

Once the tears had subsided and composure had been reestablished, we knew we had to share the news with our family. After all, treatment was imminent. My wife had convinced me that she wanted to maintain her privacy and only share her diagnosis with a small circle of family and friends. We knew we would have to inform our employers for the obvious reasons like family medical leave, insurance, and work modifications/schedules/ responsibilities. The same night we drove to her mom's home, where we had asked her sisters and brothers to meet. The sharing of the diagnosis ignited more tears and sadness among the family. I can remember, as clear as day, my wife standing in the middle of the floor holding our godson, saying to the family it will be ok. I was impressed and encouraged by her strength. At her weakest, she chose to demonstrate strength; and I was inspired by this display. We shared the news with our kids with the same emotional responses. I knew we would need a small army to help row the boat when we were at our weakest and felt like drowning. As a result, Team Mackey was born.

Believe you can, and you're halfway there.
~ Theodore Roosevelt

Chapter 4

BANG THAT DAMN GONG
Start With the End in Mind

Every cancer patient, regardless of the type of cancer, looks forward to ringing the ceremonial bell or banging the gong. This normally symbolizes the end of treatment. We were no different. So, we started with the end in mind.

My wife conducted more research than MD Anderson. She quickly became an expert and had the notes to support her learning – remember the journal. I, too, was conducting my own research, but I also took it a step further. She didn't initially approve of this approach, but later it would become a source of comfort for her. I took to the streets to ask guys I knew who had endured the process- which was too few- and spoke with women I knew were breast cancer survivors. After sharing our battle with a few friends, they quickly name-dropped female mutual friends or acquaintances I never knew were breast cancer survivors.

When engaging male friends about breast cancer in general or regarding their personal experiences, I quickly realized that there was an absence of information even if the experiences were had. In my mind, this presented a conundrum because I was well aware of the high rates of breast cancer in the United States and particularly in Mississippi. According to the Mississippi Department of Health, our state has the second-highest mortality rate in the nation. Most importantly, I know men are in meaningful relationships with these women. I present this as a sad reality, which raises more questions than I have answers: Are men simply not involved in the breast cancer battle? Do they feel uncomfortable having the discussions? Do they lack the depth of knowledge about breast cancer and are thus

reluctant to share? Is there some shame or embarrassment, or were they reluctantly sworn to privacy at the
request of their significant other, like I was? Do our
voices count, or are we unintentionally muted?

Since I referenced MD Anderson above, let me speak on
it just a bit. MD Anderson Cancer Center is as well-
known as Popeye's fried chicken. They both are the
best at what they do. Obviously, I am being a bit face-
tious, but MD Anderson (www.mdanderson.org) is
ranked the number one cancer center in the United
States. Some of you may prefer KFC or Cancer Treatment Centers of America, Church's Chicken, or your local area cancer treatment center. My point here is that
all cancer centers have been sized and measured, and
MD Anderson stands among the top to receive cancer
treatment. This does not diminish other centers at all. I
would put our doctors, nurses, and facilities up against
any. However, most dealing with a potentially life-

threatening disease would opt for treatment from the very best.

Unfortunately, MD Anderson is not a real option for most. My wife and I conducted the research, evaluated the commitment to travel out of state frequently for treatment, the insurance challenges, mental and physical exhaustion, and exorbitant supplemental costs, and concluded it was all too much to bear. Like so many, we researched our best options within the state and made sure their facility, equipment, processes, protocols, communication, treatment, staff, etc., were on par with MD Anderson's. Moreover, because we had performed the research, we could cross-reference the items above for an enhanced level of comfort that we were receiving the best treatment and service our providers had to offer.

We immediately began preparing for treatment. After the research was conducted, we had a long list of items to order. The most important items to purchase, according to my wife, were a number of logo shirts. Seriously, I was like shirts....really? I thought this to myself and would not dare say it out loud. I transformed my perspective of the shirts early on. I realized they were insignia of extreme symbolism. It was akin to soldiers dressing in army fatigues or camouflage, preparing to go to war. Those shirts created a bond and cultivated a mindset of inseparability. With our battle gear on, we knew that together we were stronger. **Lesson #1**: Men, wear the shirts with pride; or any other gear your wife or significant other may purchase. She will be eternally grateful for this minor act, and I am certain you will find much delight in the unsolicited compliments you will receive from random strangers. I sure did. I even had one lady in the Exxon gas station tell me, "You are a special man, and keep loving and supporting your wife!" I smiled *as big as day* and replied with a heartfelt thank you. This total

> **A NOTE**
>
> *"Men, remember to stay positive & supportive."*

53

stranger had recognized the brief insignia printed on my pink t-shirt that read love, hope, courage, and faith. I am confident that I walked out of the store a few inches taller than when I walked in.

I also had to purchase my wife's favorite hard candy. Again, we bought everything we knew would aid and support us in the battle. It was determined that one of my wife's chemotherapy drugs would be the Red Devil. "Excuse me, did you say, Red Devil?" Yes, Adriamycin or better known as Red Devil. How did it get such a street name? I'll talk more about this in the treatment chapter but just know that it means just what the name implies. She also received Cytoxan and Taxol Carboplatin chemotherapy treatment. The two combination treatments are referred to as the "combo" chemotherapy drugs and are equally as devastating to the body. The candy was purchased to combat the vile taste of the drugs while they were being administered. We chose the variety pack of Jolly Ranchers. **Lesson #2:**

Men, know the drugs and side effects associated with the drugs so that you may assist.

When the diagnosis becomes a reality, men must make "cancer speak" their new love language. I want to be careful not to generalize here, but I believe most women will find it attractive, sincere, and caring to witness their husband or partner immerse themselves in the research and learning jargon that will become a part of her life forever—his too. You need to speak and be well acquainted with the language: hormones, atrophy, menopause, neuropathy, port, type of cancer, type of treatment, lumpectomy, mastectomy, oncologist, prescription drug names, doctors' names, and a host of medical terminology that will create an informed individual. Conducting your own research and learning will help you navigate conversations with doctors and nurses on your wife's behalf (she will love this), allow you to have informed conversations with your wife to discuss the process, treatment, or personal care, and be able to explain the situations to family and friends without burdening your wife. Of all the new "cancer speak" words I learned, neuropathy became the one I loathed to hear the most. What is Neuropathy? Neuropathy is damage or dysfunction of peripheral nerves. It causes severe pain, burning, numbness, tingling, and weakness. In other words, when your wife is saying that her neuropathy is flaring up, you are able to empathize and offer solutions. This could be as simple as a foot or hand massage. Lastly, you will achieve a bit of confidence and humility by investing and preparing for battle with your wife or significant other. It cultivates security and unity in your relationship, which yields a wealth of benefits.

The Red Devil that was part of my wife's regiment was sure to cause neuropathy. In an effort to try to prohibit the onset and lingering lifelong effects of it, or at the very least, minimize its effect, we purchased cold-temperature gloves and socks/slippers. Once purchased, I had to freeze the gloves and slippers. This was done without fail after each treatment. Before we would go for treatment, I would pack the frozen gloves and socks with ice in my cooler. It was paramount that they remain at freezing temperature during the commute to the treatment facility and while waiting to begin treatment. My wife had read that the gloves and slippers should be placed on her hands and feet about fifteen minutes after the Red Devil was administered. She was quick to remind me it should not be 10 minutes or 20, but *15 minutes*. I did my best to oblige. So, for every treatment, without fail, I had to place these frozen gloves and slippers on my wife's hands and feet. I get chills now just thinking about the cold, about how painful that must have been to have items so cold placed on your body and could not be removed. She never complained and never spoke a negative word. The lady is a warrior, and I would go to war with her anytime. **Lesson #3**: Men, you have to be present in mind and body to contribute to the treatment and healing. I hope you heard what I said, **BE THERE!**

I lost count of the vast number of shampoos, conditioners, nail oils, body oils, vitamins, and healthy snacks my wife purchased. While I believed it to be excessive, I also knew it was very necessary. I bore witness to the realities of the Red Devil. I saw my wife fight through the loss of many of the superficial qualities that both men and women cling to, praise, desire, and lust over. **Lesson #4:** Men, physically, your wife's body may never be the same, but you better not say a single damn word to the contrary. Lift her up, compliment her, and most of all, let her know that she is loved unconditionally.

I encourage each of you at some point to look up chemo or cancer port. I found this to be one of the more gruesome practices or requirements to begin cancer treatment. Doctors make an incision on the chest adjacent to the heart. A small device or port is implanted beneath the skin. A catheter is threaded into the heart from the port. During the treatment, the port remains in the body to allow efficient and effective access to the veins for the chemo to enter the body. All liquid drugs are entered through the port. Once the skin heals over the port's access point, it becomes a bit painful to break the skin to administer treatment each week. Some cancer patients choose to leave the port in for years beyond their cancer treatment. In our case, my wife hated for the nurses to have to start an IV to draw blood for routine tests, so the port was a welcomed, less painful alternative. She complained that they could never find her veins when starting an IV. My wife did keep the port in for several months after treatment to make fol-

low-up visits less intrusive. The port made it convenient to draw blood for routine visits. This is just another
example of the mental resilience and fighting spirit that
must take root to navigate this unfamiliar path successfully.

As we continued to prepare for the mental and physical
transformations, we did not want to be shocked, surprised, or caught off guard by anything we felt we
could be prepared for. This approach led to one of the
most drastic pretreatment acts, one that would symbol-
ize a new chapter, a new fight, and a new attitude regarding our approach to this battle.

My wife had the most beautiful, long, and flowing hair.
A radiant, shiny black which she had groomed faith-
fully each week. I mean, she was serious about her hair,
and frankly, so was I. When it was down in her face
and draped across her back, it was quite an attractive
presentation. However, despite our affinity for her

hair, we decided that I would cut it off bald. I cannot overemphasize how significant this was, but we would not fall victim to the emotional rollercoaster of random patches of hair loss.

It took me some time, but I came up with the perfect symbol to minimize the haircut shock and build more courage throughout the process. I purchased a barber cape and had it screen printed

A NOTE
"Sometimes old things need to be removed to make room for the new things."

with our family motto/logo, Team Mackey, in beautiful pink lettering. As I was preparing to cut her hair, I could see how emotional she was becoming before even sitting in the chair. That's when I presented the gift. My wife's attitude and emotions immediately were replaced with feelings of love, support, and thoughtfulness. What my wife did not realize was how distraught, sad, and just how difficult it was for me to cut her beautiful black hair. I was probably more emotional than she was, but I was in battle mode and had to lead my soldier... while hurting on the inside. You never know how anyone might look when they are bald, but my wife's head was the perfect shape to magnify her beauty. Once I saw how stunning she was, I encouraged her to adopt it as her new look. Of course, she wasn't having it. That may have been a bridge too far to cross. Ultimately, our goal was achieved, which was to attack every side effect of treatment that we could to minimize its negative impact; and every resource helped in varying degrees.

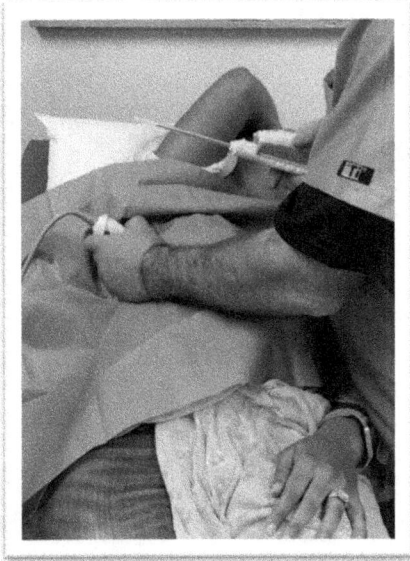

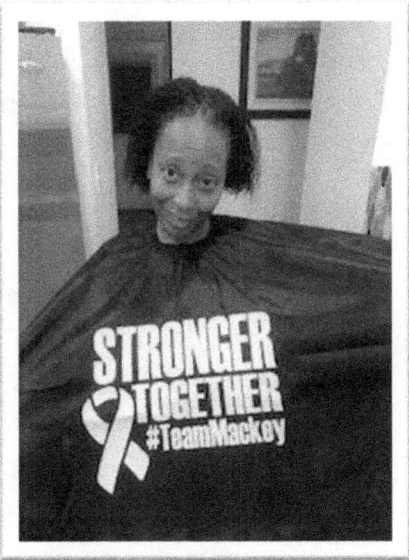

A woman is like a tea bag; you cannot tell how strong she is until you put her in hot water.

~Nancy Reagan

Chapter 5

THE TREATMENTS
Weird Science

Cancer treatments are taxing on everyone. I don't want to make it seem like those other than the cancer patient should be complaining due to their minor inconveniences. Once you witness the treatment firsthand, you quickly realize how critical your role is to the process and patient. I was fortunate, and some would say blessed, that I could contribute and support my wife at the level I did. I have always been a committed, dedicated, and accountable employee. Because I never abused my attendance and vacation days, I had more than enough leave time to dedicate to being the best wingman, partner, or soldier I could be. My job, administrator, and team provided me with flexibility, and I will always be eternally grateful. I only raise time and availability as critical pieces to the puzzle because, unfortunately, some spouses or significant others do not enjoy such luxuries at their place of employment. Once personal leave/time is exhausted, then everyone is impacted. This is only made more stressful because everyone realizes how vital employment, insurance, and a steady source of income are to ensuring cancer treatment is affordable and ongoing. **Lesson #5:** As a result, men, you absolutely must be great in other areas if your work schedule will not allow you to attend treatments. I did not say good; **GREAT** must be your standard in all supplemental tasks.

My wife qualified and completed the necessary paperwork to prove her eligibility for the Family and Medical Leave Act (FMLA) provisions at her place of employment. This was extremely helpful as she was undergoing treatment. I hate to admit this, but at the time, it never dawned on me to check to determine if I qualified for FMLA as a spouse and primary care provider during this process. Unbeknownst to me, I did. I wish I could completely blame this oversight on the human resource professional at my place of employment, but I can't. Not sure if Human Resources (HR) is required to inform me, but HR never mentioned my right to FMLA, and unfortunately, I never inquired. I was fortunate that I had the leave time available. **Lesson #6:** Men consider this lesson, every organization and business offers different benefits packages, but if your employer has more than 50 employees, you should qualify for FMLA. Employers with less than 50 should review individual state laws. Do your research, speak with your HR professional, and know your personal leave status prior to the start of the journey.

A Note

"Explore all available benefits & resources with your organization's human resource specialist."

I never missed a single treatment, twenty (20) treatments over a period of five months from January 31, 2020, to June 12, 2020. If it appears I am exhibiting boastful, proud, or sanctimonious behavior, it's because I am. In my own way, with pride, I acknowledge the significance of that timeframe and the devotion it demonstrates. Treatment was every Friday at 1:30 p.m., and it required that I be prepared and always available.

Should you not be able to make every appointment, please know that just like state and federal law, the punishment may or may not fit the crime. Ok, that's probably a poor analogy. The point I would make here is that it is vitally important that you make every treatment and doctor appointment that *you can*. Rest assured, it can and will be held against you in *her* court of law if you can make it but don't. There I go again. What I am trying to say is plan accordingly and plan ahead so that your schedule will align with her appointments, if possible.

As indicated earlier, everyone's employment status and leave policies are different; thus, allowances for missing work could mean punitive or financial disadvantages. However, if your wife or significant other is at least aware of your attempts to be present during this difficult time, you may receive a smidgen of grace. The mere fact that you are trying should encourage feelings of love and support.

Please do not think that the only reason I mention making every appointment is to pat myself on the back. I mention it also to create awareness of the broad scope of the level of commitment required to be a cancer partner. I had to ensure my professional work was always beyond reproach; take half days on each treatment Friday; pack our treatment kit (gloves, socks, candy, water, blankets, snacks, etc.); drive to treatment; wait over two hours during the treatment; cook dinner or ensure food was available that she could eat; and most importantly, be present, affectionate, and loving while she dealt with the side effects of the chemotherapy. More of the same was performed throughout the weekend as she began recovery from treatment. Nausea, fatigue, lack of appetite, and, dare I say, the mental drain are just some of the side effects that were always on full display. This is not for the faint of heart, and while most of us have heard about the cancer fight, so much is left out of the conversation.

Some would say this is a normal expectation of a spouse or significant other, but is it really, and at what level? If you feel that way, are you being subjective or objective? I submit to you that according to the limited sample of individuals that I spoke to, this was not the norm. Therefore, this may be the only time I take a written victory lap in my own honor and use those ridiculous "I" statements. I feel secure doing so on this one occasion because those who know me would vouch that I am not a vain individual. However, I wanted to highlight the enormity of what is required and, most importantly, encourage a true partnership throughout the process should you have the misfortune of a cancer diagnosis. I pray you do not. Our partnership is one key factor that I will state emphatically contributed to our success. We were down like four flat tires, like Jordan and Pippen, George and Weezy, Victor and Nikki, and Charlie and his Angels. You know, like Ashford and Simpson, we were *Solid as A Rock*!

While some may question the validity of commitment and expectations, it was so very rewarding for me to serve as the primary caretaker during our cancer battle. The experience taught me important lessons of compassion, empathy, sacrifice, and patience. It demanded that I demonstrate a positive attitude for the benefit of progress and good health. The battle showed me how to focus less on self and more on *us* and our common goals. Marriage is a mix of ups and downs, giving and receiving, tolerance and intolerance. However, when facing a common enemy like cancer, it must be about surrendering all to accomplish the shared goals and objectives of the couple. I am certain I was not doing these things 100% of the time, but it was not for lack of effort and a thoughtful attempt. So, yes, this journey was rewarding for me and ultimately transformed my thinking which I hope is more present than ever in my daily living. I hope friends and family would echo the same.

As *we* began treatment, I say *we* because of our partnership; Covid was raging across the United States. Mississippi was no different. Covid was infecting individuals at a high rate, stressing area hospitals, and causing significant health problems, even death. Because Covid was devastatingly infectious, it caused a major shutdown of businesses and organizations. It also drastically caused the health care facilities to implement restrictions on entry and access. Covid and non-Covid patients were in hospitals but could not be visited by friends and family. Sadly, many died alone. Over time, there were rare occasions where visitation was permitted; however, a host of health protocols had to be met by individuals seeking entry. Covid pandemic and resulting regulations were especially significant for us because there was no way I was going to miss a single chemotherapy treatment. I admit with some shame (not really) that we had manufactured an itty-bitty white lie to allow me to gain access to the treatment center. We told the facility staff that my wife could not function independently during her treatments and that my presence was required to carry supplies (our treatment kit), assist with bathroom breaks, and, most importantly, administer neuropathy preventive care. We did not know if my wife could do these things because she was never required to, but we did not want to risk it. Therefore, we told what I believe was a half-truth at best and an itty-bitty white lie at worst. Make no mistake, I would do it all again. I knew how important my presence and support were to maintaining our process and achieving our goals and objectives. I met all the protocols for admission into the treatment facility, and it started with me not being infected with Covid.

The Red Devil, Cytoxan, Taxol Carboplatin, and Covid could have become a deadly combination for my wife. For my wife's type of breast cancer, these chemo treatments had proven to provide the best positive response in treatment for Triple Negative. Unfortunately, they were also shown to have devastating effects on the patient. To be clear, all drugs have pros and cons or advantages and disadvantages, but the Red Devil we discovered would live up to its reputation and not just because of its bright red color. Red Devil was so destructive to the body that it could only be administered every two weeks, while the other combo treatments were administered weekly. I am still amazed that you have to be administered poison to combat this dreaded disease. Red Devil's side effects included: severe nausea, vomiting, hair loss, nail discoloration, neuropathy, mouth sores, diarrhea, fatigue, and Leukemia, to name a few.

The combo treatments replicate many of the same side effects. I remember thinking to myself that if the cancer does not kill you, the treatment certainly will. Again, the Red Devil can cause Leukemia (a significant reduction in your white blood cell count), also known as *blood cancer*. As a result of the treatment, my wife's white blood cell count became substantially low, which made her extremely susceptible and at high risk for infection. The normal white blood cell count is between 4,500 to 11,000 or 13,000 cells per microliter- attempting to remember what the doctor shared, but you can google it. At one point, my wife's white blood cell count was 1,700. It was so low that we were considering suspending treatment to allow improvement in the numbers. Dr. Young encouraged us to stay the course but to take extra precautions to avoid the risk of infection.

The extremely low white blood cell count while we dealt with Covid, one of the most transmissible infectious diseases experienced in our lifetime, was definitely cause for alarm. Keep in mind that there were only rumors of vaccines at this time, and even more, doctors and disease control experts were still puzzled about treatment options for Covid. So yes, this potential tsunami caused us significant concern. Like most, we were certain we could not afford to contract it. We had no idea if my wife's body and white blood cell count were strong enough to fight off the Covid infection. As a result, we went into super lockdown mode.

There was definitely a mask mandate in the Mackey household. Our house became a complete disinfectant zone. I was the only one that could risk going shopping for essentials because of my wife's vulnerability. I should probably share this one selfish fact that my wife was not entirely comfortable with. During the lockdown, outdoor activities significantly increased. I took this to mean that I could continue participating in my favorite hobby, pastime, or passion- golf. Hey, let's be honest, I was putting myself more at risk in Kroger and Walmart than I was on the beautiful outdoor golf courses throughout the state. We could socially distance, not have to touch any items on the course, and most importantly, I walked the course. If it seems like I am trying to

A Note

"Despite the chaos life often and unexpectedly brings, find balance and time to relax and reset. One can't be effective in life without it."

justify my continuous golfing during the pandemic, you would be correct. I believe it was the safest activity available to anyone that would allow self-protection via the CDC guidelines. Due to my golfing activity and local store runner activities, my wife insisted that I shower and change clothes immediately upon arriving home. Not just any shower, but I was told to shower with Dial soap. Considering my wife's circumstances, this was an appropriate compromise and the right and smart thing to do. Maybe a bit selfish on my part, but that temporary relief from providing care was necessary.

My wife was encouraged to continue working during treatment, but the chemotherapy and Red Devil side effects would make her daily work tasks very difficult. Dr. Young had prepared her for what was to come. That may be an overstatement, but she did inform us of what to expect. The Red Devil was notorious for exhibiting its most significant side effects on day three following treatment. Treatment was on Fridays, and of course, the dreaded third day was on Monday, as she returned to work each week. I think the side effects lasted a couple more workdays, but my wife never complained. She acknowledged the symptoms and stayed focused on her work priorities. What a Warrior! I am pretty sure most people would have taken off that third day to allow themselves time to recover. She had the medical leave time to do so and, quite frankly, had earned the right. Nevertheless, she soldiered on.

It should also be highlighted that my wife's work was in Decatur, MS. Therefore, she drove 89 miles to Jackson each Friday to attend treatment. The true test of fortitude was the 89 miles she drove back for the work-week each Sunday without fail while suffering the side effects but persevering.

As we wrapped up the treatment phase, we were thrilled to learn that the chemotherapy had significantly reduced the cyst. The Red Devil worked! We were more than thrilled. We were prayerful, thankful, grateful, and enthusiastic. Hell, you name it, if it was positive, it was a part of our reaction. Our surgical oncologist insisted that we have treatment first to determine if it would reduce the cyst, thus, reducing the amount of tissue that would have to be removed during surgery. So, treatment was the first phase we had to conquer in our prayers, planning, goals, and objectives. Suffering all the ills, mental strife, and side effects suddenly seemed worth it. For me, while experiencing all the emotions described above, I could not help but think of my mom and her battle with cancer. Although a different type of cancer and at a different stage, I was unsettled with the negative thoughts of my mom's brief remission. My mom's cancer came storming back with a vengeance, and in the process, just a few short months later, it caused her death and destroyed my optimism. I am practical enough to realize breast cancer is drastically different from lung cancer, but cancer nonetheless. All that to say, my positive and excited energy was diminished. However, there was absolutely no way I could allow my wife to glean this tainted feeling. **Lesson #7:** So, men, I did what you must do each and every day, stay positive. I did, and you should too.

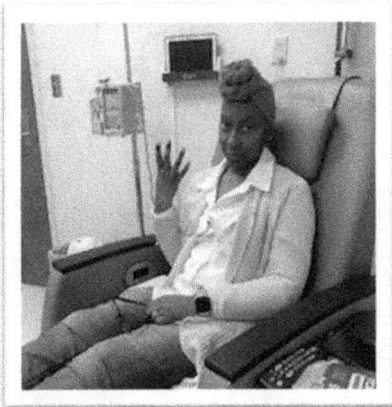

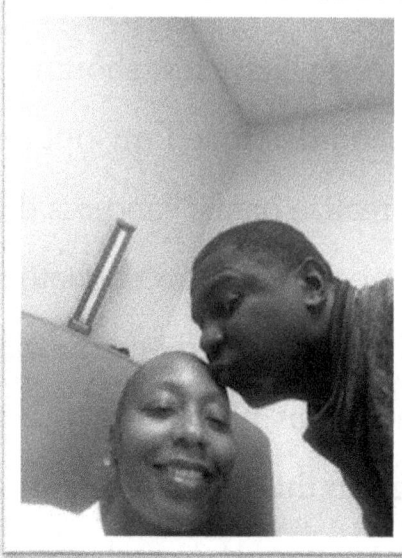
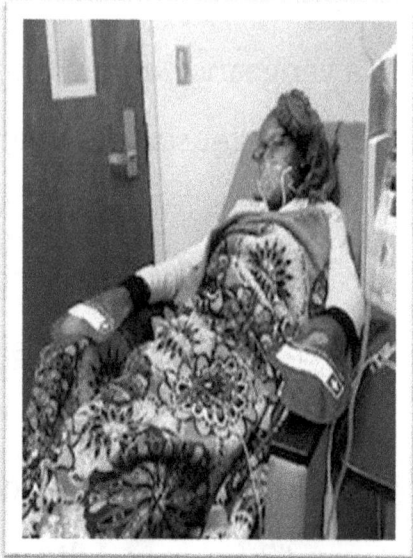
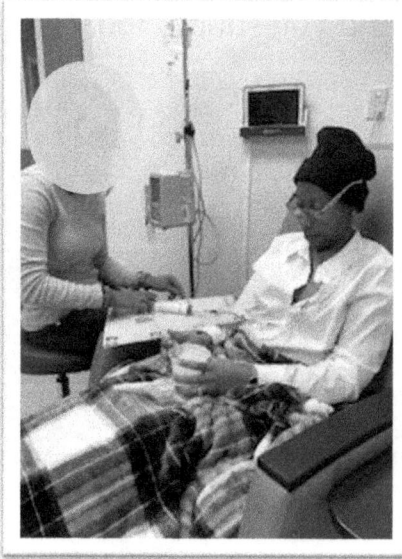
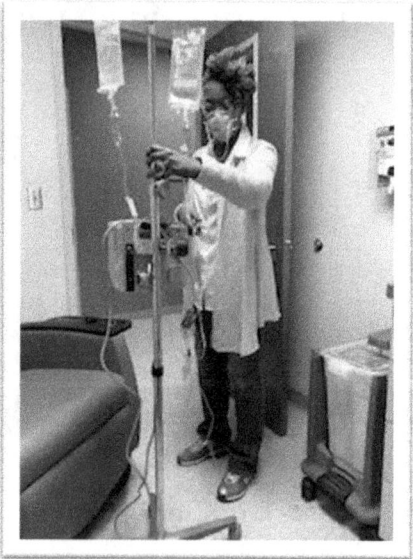

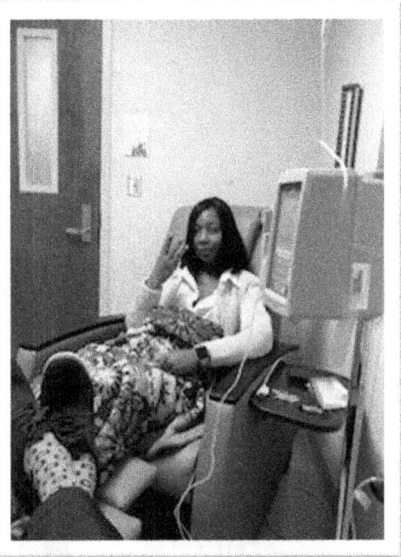

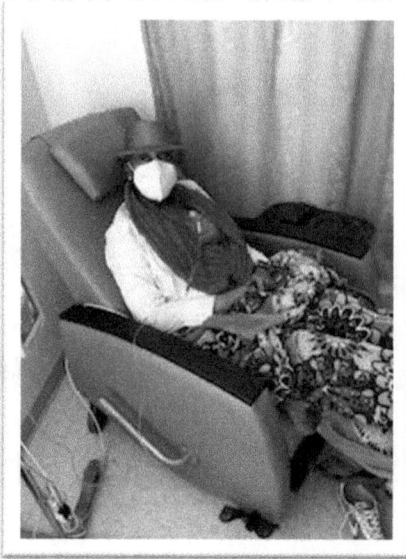

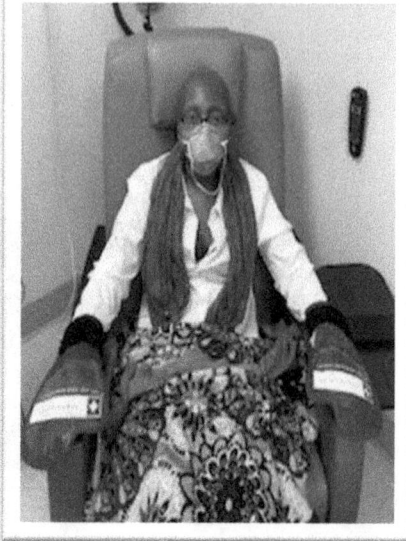

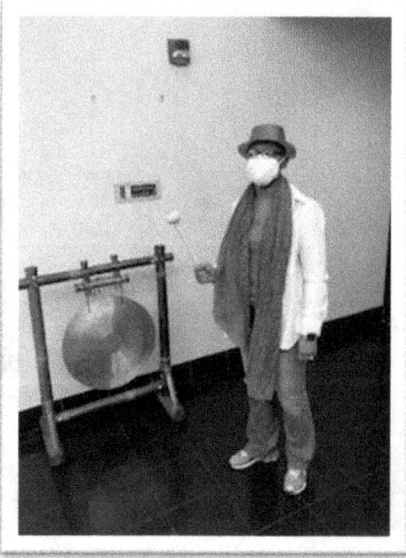

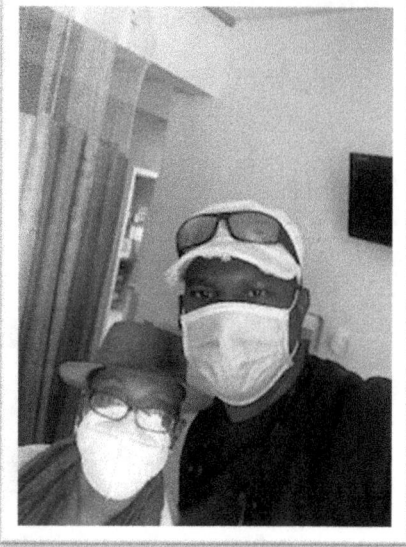

We have two options, medically and emotionally: give up or fight like hell. ~Lance Armstrong

Chapter 6

THE SURGERY
The Makings of You

After receiving our diagnosis, it was clear to both of us that we were going to have a double mastectomy. The decision was about preserving life, not a pair of breasts. Worth repeating; it was about preserving life, not a pair of breasts. I know, easy for me to say, but the life part is what I wanted us to focus on. It was almost like we were thinking the very same thing, but no one had the confidence or courage to put the option on the table. I can't remember who said what (I am sure she can), but we arrived at the same conclusion. Get rid of those mofos! We still had to see what the research said and what the doctors recommended for someone with her diagnosis. Truthfully, I don't think it would have mattered.

I referenced the research I conducted beyond Google earlier, speaking with the doctors and viewing other published sources. One of my coworkers mentioned years ago that his wife was a breast cancer survivor. He and I had a great relationship, and I knew I could speak to him privately. So, I did. He took the time to answer the many questions that I had. I can distinctly remember asking him which surgical procedure they selected. I could see the despair on his face when he stated that his wife elected to have a single mastectomy. I got the sense that they may not have agreed on this course of action, or maybe it was the best option available at that time. He mentioned that his wife was unhappy with her breast years following the single mastectomy. He said his wife hated that there was no uniformity in the size of the breast. Her breast had different angles, sizes, and shapes, and of course, the reconstructed breast was absent the natural feel. In a moment of laughter, he said the natural breast was significantly impacted by years and gravity, while the reconstructed breast looked like it would stand the test of time. We both thought this was extremely funny and laughed for quite some time. This was much-needed comic relief during an otherwise sad and dismal conversation. His last words to me were, "Get rid of them. She will be glad she did." Hearing this confirmed that we had made the right decision to have both breasts removed and reconstructed. Not only was this the healthiest option, but it also would assist with passing the vanity test.

> **A Note**
> "There are no dumb questions. You'd be amazed at the amount of information and help you can receive if only you ask."

I did not want my wife to start vacillating on our decision, so I asked my coworker if it would be ok for my wife to contact his wife to discuss all things breast cancer. Specifically, she wanted to know whether she regretted not having a double mastectomy. My friend's wife confirmed that she wished she'd had both breasts reconstructed to reduce the possibility of the cancer returning and for aesthetics. She said it was difficult to look at her breast with any level of confidence because they were so different. She went on to say that she finally had to have the other breast reconstructed to achieve the symmetry and beauty she was seeking. With that one phone call, my coworker's wife not only helped us make a pivotal decision, but her encouragement gave my wife the extra boost of confidence needed to fight the cancer battle. It was the first phone call of many, and we were and still are so grateful to her and my coworker.

Continuing with my research, I spoke to my supervisor at the time regarding my wife's condition. I was basically informing my supervisor that I would be out of the office quite a bit because my wife was beginning breast cancer treatment. The supervisor was very disappointed to learn of this news because she knew my wife personally and had a ton of respect and admiration for her. My supervisor and I shared a mutual acquaintance who had just completed treatment and reconstruction following her bout with breast cancer. I asked my supervisor if she would contact her to determine if she would entertain the notion of a call to speak with my wife. My supervisor sent a text message, and a quick response was received, encouraging the contact to be made sooner rather than later. I quickly learned that there is a network, a sisterhood if you will, of survivors who are willing and excited to be a source of inspiration to those newly diagnosed with breast cancer.

I was surprised to learn that our mutual acquaintance had just recovered from breast cancer and was not only surviving but thriving. See, I knew her quite well. Sometimes things are not always black and white. I mean that literally and figuratively. You can see a person on a regular basis and not truly know what they are going through. Matthew Canada, my pastor, would say, "People see what they see, but they don't know what they think they know." Lastly, this was a *white* lady taking time out of her day to inform, motivate and be an inspiration to my wife. The communication would happen several times throughout the process. Please forgive me because I know race is not the focus of this book; however, I would be remiss if I did not point out the irony of race in sickness and death. It is situational. Some hate people because of the color of their skin, yet they can still have the ability to love that same person when life's circumstances align the two on the same side of fate. Suddenly, race becomes the least common denominator, and concern for your fellow sister or brother becomes the priority. Therefore, throwing down your racial gloves is possible in order to fight a common enemy or no enemy at all. In this situation, the common enemy was cancer. If only we could find a positive common ground to be united indefinitely.

Ultimately, the mutual friend also confirmed the benefits of the double mastectomy. The conversations further assisted my wife in believing we were making the right decision. After speaking in detail with our surgical oncologist, we were set.

I was grateful that I had people willing to share their personal stories and connect my wife and me with others that we could lean on for information and support. The list of people we allowed to enter our circle grew, but we were focused on quality, not quantity. Quality is what we received. Remember, my wife wanted to maintain her privacy while we fought the battle. Some may have identified that I was somewhat violating our privacy pact. In my mind, the sharing was crucial to ensuring that we spoke to people who had gone through the fire. My sole motivation was to get my wife *whatever* she needed to survive this war and be the warrior I knew she would become for others fighting this same enemy. My wife was most grateful because I introduced her to a new set of acquaintances. Many became friends and still are.

The treatment successfully dissolved the cyst; however, the lymph nodes still posed a potential risk of the cancer returning. As stated above, we decided to have the double mastectomy, which would involve removing both breasts and the surrounding lymph nodes.

We arrived at the surgical center hopeful and ready to take on the procedure, but we were also fearful of the unexpected. I still wonder what was going through her mind at that moment. I had questions, but I would not dare ask. How would she react to her body without breasts? Hell, how would I? How painful would the procedure be even with the drugs? Was she scared? Question after question.

I had a moment of significant weakness after we had prepped and were awaiting the nurses to take her to surgery. I think I cried because she was so strong; and partially because I had so many questions and knew that answers would not materialize.

Our stay in the center was two days and one night. The nurses had to teach me how to provide proper postsurgical care. Honestly, in that moment, I was attempting to think beyond what was now missing and the devastation left behind. Not a pretty sight. Not a pretty sight at all. Despite it all, I somehow was able to see her total beauty. Breast be damned.

On numerous occasions, my wife had expressed dissatisfaction with the size of her breasts. She had joked that she was going to have breast surgery eventually. She, like so many, wanted to be a little bit bigger or go up a size or two. That is the casual language that was thrown around, "Up a size or two." This was all about her and her self-consciousness about her breast. I know I was not a factor in this type of thinking or decision-making because she knew that I was "not a breast man". However, I took this opportunity to once again look at the glass as half full. Trying to be positive, I suggested that the double mastectomy would provide an opportunity for her to have a new pair of breasts and achieve the size she had wanted for so long. It's possible I may have missed the mark because my sense of humor and positivity was not well received. **Lesson #8:** Men gauge your audience for your own safety. If you're like me, you're positive that you're channeling Kevin Hart, but to her, you're being a jerk... a sarcastic one at that. I'm still not sure I was wrong, especially since she is a little bigger now. Ironically, she does not like the newly reconstructed bigger breasts. It is worth noting here for women that if you do not like the newly constructed breasts, it is very likely that your husband or significant other will adopt the same position. Be mindful that you both, at some point, are going to try to return to some semblance of lustful attraction. Your positive attitude can go a long way toward accomplishing this objective. So, ladies, embrace the new breasts. It will encourage your husband or partner to do the same.

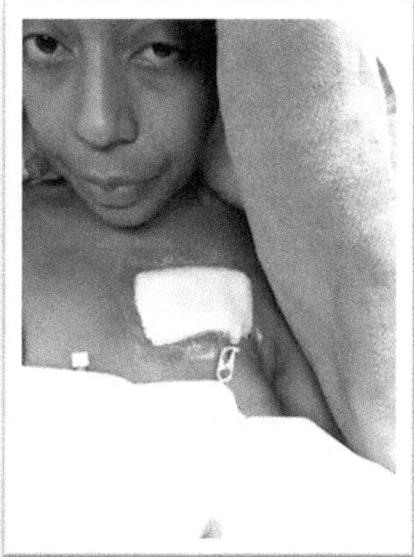
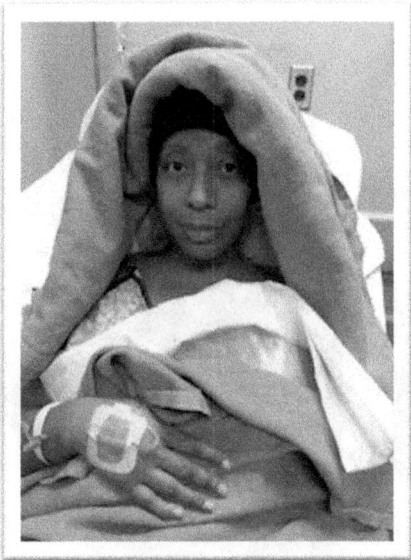
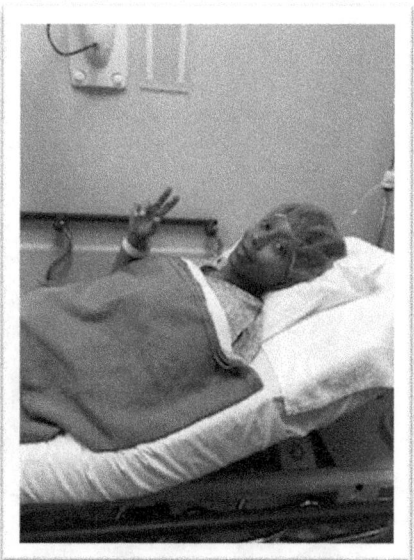

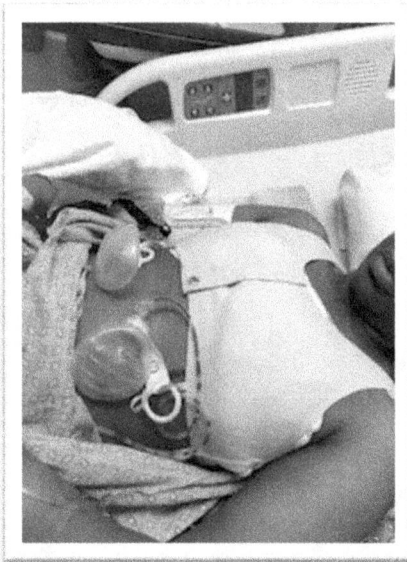

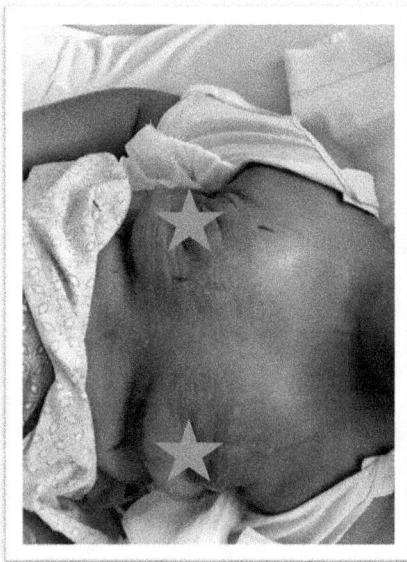

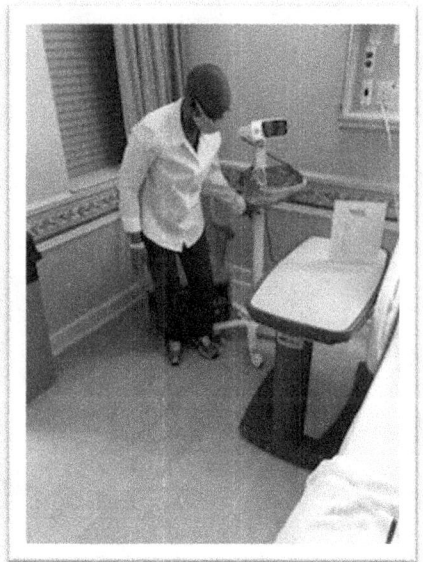

He who has a why to live can bear almost any how.

~Friedrich Nietzsche

Chapter 8

THE "D" WORD
Til Death Do Us Part...

Say it. You might as well go ahead and say it now because ignoring it, not saying it, or making up some catchy acronym to diminish it will not make its reality disappear. I'm not sure how often one thinks of life and death. Personally, I quickly dismiss the thought of death and try to focus on living life to the fullest in every positive way possible. I think the same is true for health. It is not really given much consideration until annual wellness exams, for those who are health-conscious, or your actual health starts to fail you in some capacity. When I hear the word cancer, I immediately connect *health* and *death*. Living an exciting and invincible life, you don't expect to be impacted early on by either; but you also know that dysfunction in one can, unfortunately, lead to the other. I know this sounds extremely negative and even insensitive to some; however, you think and act differently when you have lost as many as I have in my family to cancer.

As stated, my family is no stranger to cancer and cancer deaths. By my count, and I must admit that I am the worst at chronicling dates, times, people, and places, but I am fairly confident my dad has lost three brothers to cancer, and my mom has lost one sister and two brothers to cancer. My mom's passing on May 29, 2019, would make it four on her side of the family. I am also painfully aware of a host of other cousins and family members that have passed from cancer. Let me say clearly, that I am sure this is not my family's experience alone, but rather this happens all too often- to way too many families.

It has been my experience that the grief and emotional toll of losing a family member to cancer are impacted by the nature of the relationships. In other words, based on the type of family relationship, kinship status, or general closeness, it is evident that one can expect a different emotional reaction to losing a family member to cancer. If we are honest about it, your relationship with the cancer patient will determine your emotional reaction or if there is any reaction at all. For example, when a friend, distant relative, or coworker passes from cancer, there is a feeling of sympathy for the family, empathy for those closest (immediate family), compassion, and a mutual feeling of heartache for their loss. However, the emotional impact is much different, much greater, more significant,

A Note
"Death is both a reality & inevitability, so be present and cherish the NOW moments you have with your loved ones."

and overwhelming the closer the kinship and relation-ship. Seems pretty straightforward, but the reality is that it is just not that simple.

When I first learned of my mom's cancer diagnosis, I was in a state of shock, a helpless, fearful state of shock. I guess I probably should not have been since my mom was a smoker all of her adult life, but nonetheless, the emotional toll was extremely heavy to bear. It was only magnified when the family learned that she was in Stage IV, and the dreaded spread had begun. Realists will take stock and know that the end is near. Fre-quently, we are reminded that science and medicine can overshadow and seem to defeat the prayers and prayerful. In short, too often, cancer wins, causing us all to lose.

The cancer battle is drastically different from a parent to a child than that of a spouse to spouse. The love - while the same - is different, the treatment is a mixed bag based on diagnosis, but what is required for supervision, protection, and personal treatment, I will argue, are vastly different. Follow me. As a son, my expectations were different from that of a husband. As a son, the sensitivity, thoughtfulness, and supervision experiences felt natural. The love, comfort, and attention were easy and were given without regard for personal sacrifices. A number of books have been written to describe this situation, focusing primarily on dealing with the emotional, financial, and spiritual struggle. Yet, the literature is a bit minimal concerning spouse-to-spouse interaction, especially from the perspective of a male, even more, a black male traveling this spontaneous, irrational and bizarre journey. As a result, I found myself answering the call to provide a unique perspective when breast cancer attacks, and the husband is required to play a pivotal role that requires passion, commitment, patience, and love. This in itself was a process.

Psychology teaches that there are five stages to processing grief. They are denial, anger, bargaining, depression, and acceptance. With zero hesitation, I can confirm this as fact. The significance here is that no matter how strong you are, when a spouse hears the dreaded words, "You have cancer," their mind is flooded with thoughts of their loved one dying. You would not be human if you didn't. My intent here, however, is to encourage you that while this is a normal and almost expected reaction, don't stay in that place. Indeed, to stay in that mindset of dread will do nothing but secure your defeat. Please believe your sick spouse will pick up on it as well. **Lesson #9**: My advice is don't be so focused on death that you allow your hope, your faith, or your strength to die before the fight ever starts. You owe it to yourself and your spouse! Again, say it, call it by its name, so the bastard knows you mean business and that you are not going down without a fight! Say it with me, "Death to cancer! Cancer Sucks! Period!"

It's not whether you get knocked down,

it's whether you get up. ~Vince Lombardi

Chapter 9

YOUR WORDS HAVE POWER
Power to Heal and Power to Kill
Power to Build Up and Power to Tear Down

About two years after completing treatment, my wife stated, and I quote, "I am just starting to feel close to you." Those words would ordinarily not cause alarm; however, nearly two years had passed. That's right, two. I laid there in the bed, trying to process what the hell had just been stated to me. I was bewildered, and I was not sure how to feel, quite honestly. However, those words were *profound, illuminating, and disheartening.* The words were profound because they spoke of an abstract concept of closeness that I would be hard-pressed to define. I could not weigh in or respond to the comment, partially because I am certain our definitions and expectations of closeness differed.

It was profound because she felt this way and demonstrated the courage to verbalize it to me. Even more, I had to, at that moment, understand why or how she would possibly feel this way. Ultimately, I did not respond because I knew my response would be taken out of context, thus possibly negatively impacting this new closeness she now felt. Profound, in that, I did not have a damn clue!

Regardless of where I believed our marriage and love to be, my wife had definite thoughts of her own. This was critical, and I am not trying to overstate this for effect, but I wondered what level of closeness did we share prior to this rekindling of sorts. What level of dysfunction had brought this on? Was this my own doing, or was this a result of my wife's insecurities and negative behavior serving as the catalyst? Those two adjectives are very powerful and could represent a method of deflecting any personal responsibility; however, I had nothing to draw from. It was illuminating because

I had a plethora of questions without the possibility of obtaining any answers.

In truth, what she said was not only disheartening but a little embarrassing for me. You know how it feels when you think you did a good job, only to find out that you actually failed miserably and did not have a clue as to why? That was this magnified by ten. After all the many sacrifices, encouragement, expressions of love, and experiences of vulnerabilities, I could not help but feel disappointed. Yes, it was disheartening, to say the least. I laid there and pondered how she arrived at this new closeness and what had I done to provoke it, support it, and how in the hell do I sustain it? Yet, in reality, I could not move beyond three real questions that were squarely the source of my bewilderment and heartbreak. When did she lose the closeness? How did she lose the closeness? Why the heck hadn't I noticed?

Nothing will be the same. **Lesson #10:** Men, be prepared for variations and levels of this to occur in every aspect of your relationship or marriage. Your wife or significant other may give the impression that things are normal, but rest assured that she will be battling the emotional scars of breast cancer, which go far beyond her physical breasts and body. The scars are present but suppressed while she makes sense of her new normal. That includes you. The fact that I was unaware that our closeness had deteriorated and persisted in that state for nearly two years should not have shocked me. Again, keep in mind that she was experiencing raw emotions like heartbreak, embarrassment, depression, and disappointment; and knowing that she was still in a very vulnerable place, I wasn't shocked by her feelings. Men, you will discover that it is important to celebrate the fact that she was able to acknowledge the issue and that there was a level of resolution to return to what was once held dear to the relationship or marriage- communication and closeness. That is all that mattered, and my silence allowed her to feel comfortable sharing. **Lesson #11:** To achieve long-term growth, you must learn to sometimes temporarily conceal your personal feelings. What do I mean? Be mindful of how you respond. This is pivotal. I admit this can seem contradictory, but it is very necessary. Silence can yield positive results. Remember I told you early on that my friend told me to "Just shut the hell up and don't say anything; just listen because not sh*t you say will be right." This was one of those moments I realized he was right. Specifically, I mean there is a time and space to respond, not to respond, or just to listen and receive. Learn and know the difference.

As I write this section, I am still having difficulty adequately putting into words what my wife shared with me. I don't know how to explain exactly what I was feeling, but I felt I needed to be the very best version of myself. I can only guess that my wife was reflecting on the brief time that we had been married. We were married on December 12, 2018, and she was diagnosed less than a year later. She made the statement, "You didn't sign up for this." I am not sure why I had both perception and awareness at that moment, but I immediately recognized that those words, if not responded to properly, could destroy the very foundation our marriage was built upon. I responded by saying, "I love you, and I meant it when I said for better or worse, in sickness and in health. Don't ever say that again."

As men, we tend to say things sometimes, not realizing the true power of our words. Most of the time, we have absolutely no intent to disrespect, demean, or hurt our spouses or significant other. Despite our intentions, our words can still cut hard and deep. Considering your wife's vulnerable and emotional state, it is important to have a keen awareness of what you say and how you say it. For once, you will be forced to think differently and interpret your wife or significant other's words in a new and unfamiliar way. Before you speak a single word, determine if you are better off remaining silent for the benefit of both parties. If not silent, then be mindful not to make a single negative comment. Ultimately, she cannot criticize you for words never spoken. However, she will find it difficult to erase the stain of degrading, inconsiderate, or hurtful language. This rings true for words, tone, and intent. Silence in these situations can do no harm. Wives likewise must be careful not to confuse his silence with avoidance. You will learn that silence is wisdom in operation that gives you both an opportunity to stop, reset, and think before you speak. Unfortunately, *"once it's out there, there's no taking it back."*

A Note
"Part of what makes communication effective is our ability to adapt and adjust our language to fit new situations."

I hope you are able to ascertain how demanding, stressful, and painful the battle can be from reading about our personal journey. To fight these battles on uncommon ground, without your partner squarely by your side, and with any impressions of wavering support, I would argue, is detrimental to treatment, successful outcomes, and, dare I say, the relationship or marriage. So be there and be accounted for. I promise she will remember, appreciate, respect, and love the one who walked through the fire with her.

My wife and I were watching one of our favorite sports shows (ok, maybe one of my favorite sports shows that she just happens to tolerate). Being very fond of one of the sport's hosts, I commented that the show's female host looked as if she had gained a little weight. This comment was probably unnecessary and would be insensitive if the sports host could hear me. I should probably note that my wife can name all of my famous superstar crushes, and I could likewise name hers. However, without hesitation or a second thought, my wife, in a very definitive and defensive voice, stated, "As if that is a bad thing." Her defensiveness caught me by surprise. Was this a misfire on my part?

On another occasion, we had a similar account play out regarding her hair. As previously described, my wife had this beautiful, thick, long-flowing black hair. I, on occasion, would jokingly question how she achieved the depth of the color, insinuating that the color came out of a bottle. However, that's not relevant here. After many months post-treatment, my wife's hair began to grow back. Remember, my wife's head and unique facial features made her the perfect candidate to rock the short hair going forward. In other words, even if she could grow twenty inches of length, I now preferred the shorter hair look. I thought it made her look uniquely beautiful and attractive. The new hair growth was forming, and I could tell she was excited about it. So was I. Equally, it was etched in my mind how difficult it was for us to decide to cut it all off even though we knew it was the best course of action. The hair's new growth can take on many forms in terms of texture, color, and style. The patient has zero control of either of these attributes early on. The hair is in a perpetual 'wait and see stage' or a take what you can get situation. Once the chemo leaves the body, the natural hair rejuvenation occurs. At least you hope so. Our research did identify cases where permanent alopecia did result.

Why am I making such a big deal about hair, hair loss, and hair growth? Well, anyone who pays the slightest bit of attention to any woman will recognize that her hair is a big deal. I mean, a BIG deal. Even after saying it twice, it is an understatement on my part. My wife went to the beauty salon to get her hair perfectly styled every Friday or Saturday. Something to the tune of about $85 to $150 weekly, depending on the services rendered. Hair was a big damn deal. Well, after her hair started growing back, I noticed her excitement and happiness. Knowing how my wife once loved getting her hair styled and cared for, I suggested – and it went something like this, "Baby, you should start back going to the beauty salon and start getting your hair styled." That's right, I am a total thoughtful package. So I thought. Out of nowhere, without hesitation or a second thought and in that same definitive and defensive tone she had used when talking about the weight gain of the female sport's host, she asked, "Oh, so you don't like my hair?"

In my Kevin Hart voice, I'm like, "No no no no no no no!" This was a moment I could opt for silence, but I thought further explanation would be much more beneficial, even necessary. After reiterating how much I loved her new short hairstyle, I tried to explain that I wanted her to get back into a routine of self-care and doing the things she enjoyed that gave her confidence and demonstrated self-love. It had very little to do with the actual hair per se, but more to do with her progressing back to a better place, where I thought she was most happy. I tried to explain, but I do not think my explanation was well received.

In hindsight, I believe my wife knew that I was being thoughtful, genuine, and speaking from a place of love, respect, and support. However, my wife's reaction to the general statement about the female sport's host weight gain and my suggestion that she go to the beauty salon was symptomatic of a much more complex and significant problem: a loss of self-confidence. **Lesson #12:** Men, you will see your wife or significant other's body undergo significant transformation caused by the chemo treatment. Unfortunately, none of it is positive. It is further complicated when they have to suffer the removal of their breast with the anticipation of having them reconstructed. I understand that only my wife, other breast cancer patients, or cancer patients, in general, can truly lend voice to the mental and physical impacts of the body transformation and loss of self-confidence that one experiences. To complicate things even more, they may begin to speculate and agonize over how their spouse or partner honestly perceives them. They question whether their spouse will ever look at them the same, be attracted to them again, or love them the same. These may seem like strange questions, but they are a common byproduct of the process, and only a fool would not take stock. It leads to comments like the one my wife made, "You did not sign up for this." It leads to insecure statements and feelings, causing many things to be taken out of context. If not wise in your approach, it can lead to unnecessary arguments that only contribute to what we hope is temporary self-loathing and insecurity.

Lesson #13: Men, you must become very vigilant in your understanding, learning, compassion, communication, and expressions of love and support. Your wife or significant other sits on a very slippery slope, and for some, your attitude can go a long way towards their full recovery. You must find a way to do the small things bigger, compliment everything often, and go the extra mile to express your love and support. I will give you an example. As my wife was preparing to return to work after treatment, I knew she was unhappy with her physical appearance. I mentioned hair loss, but the loss extends beyond the head to every part of the body — specifically, my wife lost her eyelashes and eyebrows. My wife has big beautiful brown eyes, which is one of her most attractive features to me (just saying). However, when your eyes draw attention to your face (and hers most certainly do), and

> **A Note**
> *"Don't be afraid to express your need to be affirmed and validated by your sick spouse while on this journey."*

you don't have eyelashes or brows, it can be an awkward or embarrassing existence. So, I elected to do a bit of research and discovered temporary tattoo eyebrows. I expedited my order while hoping I had the right size and shape. Not only did I research and order the eyebrows, but I also took the liberty to put them on each week without fail until her eyebrows grew back in naturally, a few months after completing chemo.

This simple act demonstrated compassion, awareness, and support. It contributed to her regaining confidence in her physical appearance. She appreciated the sensitivity demonstrated, and I was delighted in her happiness. **Lesson #14:** Look for your opportunities to do the same. It will contribute to significant independent victories until the next battle while you fight the ongoing war. In short, a little thoughtfulness and initiative can pay big mental and spiritual dividends.

"When the inner beauty exceeds the outward beauty–

it creates a magical dance in the heart."

~Angie Karan

Chapter 10

YOU A SUPERFICIAL DUDE
Shallow Hal or Not

Famous comedian Dave Chappelle had a segment on his comedy series many years ago called "When keeping it real goes very wrong." Let me begin by saying that breast cancer is about the success of ultimate survival and sometimes the most unfortunate death. But, if you are fortunate (or blessed) to be a survivor, you must prepare for the humanistic elements of the cancer battle. Just like hair loss, changes the body goes through will have a significant impact on both the patient and spouse or significant other. To better understand this dilemma, I have created four body transformation stages: pre-diagnosis body, treatment body, pre-surgery body, and post-surgery body. Furthermore, by *keeping it real*, we do not lose sight of one of this book's objectives: to help spouses or significant others anticipate and effectively cope with the body's physical transitions that will absolutely occur as a result of the chemotherapy.

The four body transformations are considerably self-explanatory; however, for context, allow me to explain why I have identified these stages as significant to the cancer battle. Pre-Diagnosis Body is the size, shape, and weight women have prior to any cancer-related changes. During this stage, most ladies are confident and reassured in their looks, although you may hear them say they want to lose weight, tone up a little bit, or something generic but minimal. Treatment Body represents a drastic departure from the pre-diagnosis body because the chemotherapy begins to cause alterations to their body. As I stated earlier, the patient begins to lose their hair; the

> **A Note**
> "Real love has depth far surpassing the notion of "skin deep." The deeper your love, the stronger your bond."

fingernails and toenails become dark and brittle; the skin's complexion takes on different variations, there is scarring from the surgical port installation; the treatments cause mild to significant weight loss or gain (specific to the body's response), and their walk may change due to the pain associated with the neuropathy. The Pre-Surgery Body consists of all the features mentioned above and has the added body transformation brought on by the surgical procedure (lumpectomy, mastectomy, a combination of the two, or maybe a procedure I am unfamiliar with).

Lastly, there is the Post-Surgery Body, which consists of all the above; however, at this juncture, breast reconstruction should have occurred, and your body is beginning to resemble the pre-diagnosis body phase.

Each stage carries a unique set of emotions and reactions for both the wife and spouse or significant other. Again, I cannot adequately add value to what my wife or any cancer patient must feel as these transformations occur, but based on her comments, she suffered a significant loss of self-confidence and security. I can understand this change in attitude. Most men who fight this battle with their wives or significant others will witness the body transformation firsthand. You sympathize because you have witnessed the body's devastation and pray and hope for the day when recovery is complete and pleasing to your wife. This may seem a bit insensitive, but this book, if nothing else, is honest, pure, and transparent. As an eyewitness, you can never unsee what you saw. It requires a strong love and appreciation for your wife's mental, spiritual, and physical self so that you may remain or regain that lustful attraction. The superficial dude will find this place difficult to discover, but the unconditional loving dude will see it as a temporary setback. It can be done. I am a living witness.

Regardless of how much you try to provide assurances, it will not stop your wife or significant other from wondering if her appearance is pleasing to you. Look and listen for signs that she has embraced the outcomes of her new post-surgery body. This is vitally important because it will rebuild confidence and security as well as restore her outlook on her own attractiveness. Husbands or significant others must be at their very best in providing reassurance. In short, do not let a superficial you diminish progress made in her physical or mental recovery and renaissance.

Lastly, as a man, see it, process it, and try to find comfort or peace instead of casting superficial judgments that could linger beyond the treatment and surgery. At this juncture, being a superficial dude is your worst enemy, leading to internal grief and potential destruction of the relationship or marriage. The Bee Gees' song asks, "How deep is your love?" Think about it.

There is a season for everything under the sun—even when we can't see the sun. ~ Jared Brock

Chapter 11

PREPARE FOR THE DROUGHT
*Business **Not** as Usual*

From diagnosis, to the final treatment, through the reconstructive surgery, and post-surgery physical and mental challenges, months or even years may pass. Men or significant others need to be prepared to hunker down on the intimacy front. A drought is coming. The reader should be reminded of some obvious disclaimers here. First, I think it is safe to say that every couple's sex life is different, and I am certainly not claiming to be a sex expert. I also suspect that if you had a healthy sex life prior to a cancer battle, it is safe to say there is a considerable possibility of returning to that point. It may also be safe to say that if you previously had a healthy sex life, your intimacy may not have declined during the phases identified. However, the latter is very difficult to imagine.

A safe assumption can be made regarding sex during the cancer battle- it will occur less frequently, if at all. **Lesson #15:** As men, we need to be aware of this possibility and understand the reasons why. I believe that knowing the why and communicating it frequently is extremely important. I have shared with you the many challenges associated with an ongoing cancer battle. I do not think it is necessary to repeat those here, but I will acknowledge that those very reasons can and will diminish your wife's sexual appetite. Men tap out because of a long day at work, a minor illness, or insignificant emotional trauma. Well, imagine the mental hurdle a woman must overcome while enduring cancer treatment, surgery, healing, and pain. I suspect the last thing on their mind is sexual activity. Yes, even with the one they love and desire. Men must acknowledge that the drought exists not because women want it to but because the obstacles are too great to participate mentally and physically. Here again, this is why it is vitally essential that the cancer patient communicate their reasons and feelings with their spouse or partner regarding the decrease in sexual activity to avoid unnecessary conflicts or preventable hurt feelings.

The drought could persist for an indefinite timeframe, and even when activity resumes, you should be prepared for changes. The neuropathy causes pain, weakness, and numbness in primarily the hands and feet. I would add knees to the list. These side effects can affect sexual positions, duration, and hand strength, causing a host of other restrictions. Even more, many mental obstacles and body confidence issues can influence your intimacy. I like to think of it as a new intimacy with minor adjustments and variations. Here again,

nothing that frequent and transparent communication cannot
resolve. I would also encourage
the patient to lead and initiate
these conversations because it
will demonstrate recognition
and provide reassurances that

> **A Note**
> "During intimacy
> droughts, find other
> ways to experience
> & inspire closeness
> until those moments
> of passionate recon-
> nection can occur."

only she can. No one wants to feel the sting of rejection.
These conversations should occur throughout the journey, especially once you are in remission, if you have
any hopes of maintaining a healthy sex life. I am certain
we can all agree that intimacy is pivotal to a healthy relationship or marriage.

Let me attempt to go a bit deeper without being redun-
dant but relevant. This is likely the most confusing and
challenging conundrum opposing your efforts to reig-
nite and sustain your intimacy. Moreover, it is a difficult proposition. At the moment when your wife or sig-

nificant other may feel their lowest and lack the confidence to value and reveal their new body, new energy, assertiveness, and sexiness is needed the most. What does this look like in real life? Well, your spouse or significant other has seen your body in its most vulnerable state. In fact, if he has performed his marital responsibility, he has provided bodily care that could impact how the body is regarded going forward. So, at the moment, when you need the arousal response of your wife's touch, sexiness, and an illuminating confidence, you receive neither. Honestly, it may now be nonexistent, thus leaving the spouse or significant other to use their imagination and creativity to have an active sexual relationship with their partner. Everyone is different, but this could potentially go on for months and even years.

Trying to reconnect sexually is only made worse when she has no desire for any level of intimacy. This is a point you and your spouse want to focus your energy on trying to avoid. **Lesson #16:** Men, this is why you must uplift, compliment, support, and speak positive affirmations of her attractiveness so that she knows that your desire remains strong and passionate. She absolutely must know that you love her post-surgery body as much as you did the pretreatment body. Make no mistake, this could be the eventual lifeline you both need to reconnect and possibly end the remnants of the drought.

"Once you choose hope, anything is possible."

~Christopher Reeve

Chapter 12

THE OTHER "D" WORD
Depression Sucks

Keep in mind that your wife can have successfully beat cancer and be celebrating her remission, yet the battle will rage on as she seeks to gain confidence and stability in her body and mental composition. For us, it has been over two years, and we are still trying to put the pieces together. This is when I believe that whatever your wife is experiencing is the most revealing. Why? Because it has become less about physical cancer itself and more about its mental, spiritual and emotional effects. These feelings become more pronounced and demand greater patience on your part.

In the spirit of moving on and accepting our blessing of remission, patience and understanding are a little more challenging to extend. This is when you wish for the very best, the conviction, the confidence, the self-reliance, and boldness, which is her true self, to emerge. Sadly, there was a period when she was experiencing self-loathing, helplessness, and self-pity. These are persistent foes to our forward movements, yet we continue towards our goal. If I am honest, I am ready to move on to the next chapter and embrace the newness that has been provided by surviving a challenging set of life lessons.

> ### A Note
> "Watch for prolonged silence, isolation, loss of appetite, moodiness, or constant crying. It's more than a difficult day or PMS. Depression is a serious medical behavioral health condition that requires professional help."

When all is said and done, you may encounter the dreaded "D" word if the helplessness persists. Yes, unfortunately, depression. Not a debilitating depression, but one that is functional and cannot be detected by most. However, it is experienced in raw and rare form in the home. My wife is one of the strongest, most disciplined, most intelligent, most dedicated, and most considerate people I know, so it was difficult for me to understand and accept her brief encounter with depression. Was I the cause? How can I be a part of the solution? Is it temporary? Moreover, how do we achieve a full recovery beyond the depression? All valid questions which still don't have answers. To date, this remains a mystery to me because I constantly wonder about the cause and can only speculate on what is not being said. Even worse, I may have to decode what is actually being said. I could chalk it up to two people speaking two very different cancer love languages.

Dealing with my wife's depression was difficult for me. I witnessed cancer's physical and mental destruction daily during treatment and surgery. I had a unique vantage point to reference the negative emotions and thoughts. I could sympathize with the physical transformation of her body. These things I knew she had absolutely no control over. It was a part of the grieving and growing process of cancer, another battle. It took some time for me to discern my wife's cancer battle and the battle with depression while in remission. While in remission, I thought the focus would automatically revert to us living and loving as a happily married couple. I wanted nothing but good vibes for my wife, marriage, and home. Unfortunately, I did not have a clue how to get there.

I needed to differentiate between my wife's battle with cancer and her recovery to make sense of it all. I felt that I had given all of me to her during the battle against cancer. I was in the trenches, firing and fighting like hell. I prepared for the treatments, attended the treatments, was by her side for every appointment, shopped for groceries, cooked or provided all the meals, provided the in-home medical care, and showered her with affection, love, and support. I was a dedicated and determined soldier. We had fought this battle together like soldiers. Like a soldier, I believed it to be my sworn duty to love and cover my wife. Unfortunately, like a real soldier who returned home after the war, my wife had difficulty transitioning back to normal life. Things had changed; she had changed. Excuse the analogy, but it is the closest example to what I believe actually resembles a type of cancer, Post-Traumatic Stress Disorder (PTSD).

Experiencing this new battle left me puzzled and feeling like part of the problem, with no possibility of being a part of the solution. My wife was suffering in silence. Silence nor communication seemed to resolve the situation. In fact, conversations began to get short, consistent with my patience, on a daily basis. If not for my circle of friends, supporters, and golf, I believe we would have dissolved to nothing. But, I was determined that would not be the complete story. It was witnessing her battle back from the horrific cancer circumstances. It was her strength and perseverance. It was my ability to discern that there was a greater cause. Acknowledgment and consideration of her determination demanded a little, no, a lot of grace as she fought each battle. It was my prayer. It was my love for this woman. This same love made me realize that we needed to seek professional help if we were going to endure and survive the war. We had fought many skirmishes, but it appeared that we would have to win one more battle to win the war: professional counseling. I had reservations, I had doubts, but most of all, I'd had enough of the negative state that was becoming our existence. I can now state without reservation that counseling works. Well, only if you both want it too. A good counselor can provide a safe space to vent, ask questions, laugh, cry, and dialogue about the critical issues at the core of the problem. I confirmed some of my assumptions, learned of fears (perceived and real), and heard her speak unfiltered, which I had longed for.

Most importantly, I realized that I was not as great as I had self-proclaimed. Well, let me put it like this, I learned that I was great at what I had done, but there was so much more that she felt could have been done. I found myself feeling guilty for the time I spent away from the house on the golf course. What I am uncertain of is if she understood that golfing was my temporary peace and a place to hit the reset button. This peace allowed me to continue to provide care without regret, contempt, or malice. Counseling allowed me to share my approach and hope it was received with the desired intent. Counseling works. I have seen progress. I have seen self-confidence boosted. I have witnessed awareness and thoughtfulness. Thankfully, I see the depression fading.

Lesson #17: Men and their partners should be mindful and aware that healing is an ongoing process for you both. You deceive yourself if you believe you have gotten by without unseen injuries and battle wounds that are all healed. There is no timeline, just trust the process. The path is not linear, directional, or without caution lights. It is, of course, individual, and attitudes will vary; however, counseling can be a means to resolution and peace. It can generate thought and conversation. It can help you see actual realities and eliminate false expectations. Be open-minded- be counseled.

"Watch your thoughts, they become words; watch your words, they become actions; watch your actions, they become habits; watch your habits, they become character; watch your character, for it becomes your destiny." ~Frank Outlaw

Chapter 13

THE EMOTION OF IT ALL
Giving You the Best That I Got

It's often said that men have a hard time expressing deep personal emotions. There may be an element of truth to that. May I submit that we simply express ourselves differently from women. For me, I find music an ideal vehicle for expression. In the '80s, Anita Baker had a hit song called *Giving You the Best That I Got*. The lyrics perfectly express what my heart wanted to say and what my mind wanted to do:

*"The scales are sometimes unbalanced
And you bear the weight of all that has to be
I hope you see that you can lean on me
And together, we can calm a stormy sea
We love so strong and so unselfishly
And I tell you now that I made a vow
I'm giving you the best that I got, baby."*

Frequently, I would look at my wife and wish I knew exactly what she was thinking and how she really felt. I am keenly aware that she was never as good as she stated she was or as she shared. I felt that she genuinely desired to be mentally and physically in the positive place that she communicated to me; however, I don't think the chemo and pain from the surgery would allow her to exist there. I was also convinced that she wanted to maintain a positive attitude for me. I believed that my mental and physical well-being was also a part of the internal battle she was fighting. She wanted to shield and protect me from the indirect spouse cancer battles as best she could. I suppose it is also possible she did not believe I would understand or that it was too much to comprehend. Maybe she thought I was not in a position to help or that discussions would be void and meaningless. Who knows? Regrettably, I think that involved lying about the need for assistance, her level of pain, and her general dispo-

sition. Despite the days when conversation was over-
flowing or days when silence seemed to be the best temporary drug, I am resolute in thinking that I (we) will
never know what our wives or significant others are
truly thinking or feeling. This is a sad reality. However,
our "positive" presence somewhat supersedes. It is sincerely the best medicine we as spouses or significant
others can offer.

How do the silence or polite lies manifest themselves?
How do you cope with or provide care and support for
the unknown? You are left to your own vices. I'm not
sure if she cares at that moment because she feels her
situation and needs are much greater. Furthermore,
she is right. This is when you must move in silence, to
the exclusion of her but for her. If you must communicate, be succinct. This approach worked well for my
wife, but you must be prepared to fill the void when
your partner loves mindless banter. Always keep in

mind that it's okay to stop talking and offer hugs and kisses.

I would watch her at what I believed were some of her lowest moments and become overwhelmed with emotion because I knew she was not in a good place. As a husband who swore to protect, provide for, and cover his wife, I felt emasculated and neutered in those situations. This helpless feeling goes beyond duties and tasks. You want to take the pain away or somehow share in it to lighten the burden. Even though you realize it is a process that only she can overcome, you cannot help but ask yourself why. Why Lord?

My wife had Triple Negative Breast Cancer, and as previously stated, this type of breast cancer has the highest reoccurrence rate. While you are grateful for every day in remission, I am saddened by the thoughts or potential that we may have to someday prepare for battle again. This is our indefinite reality. While difficult, I have discovered that your attitude and thinking must not succumb to such negative forces. You realize how blessed and fortunate you are to have won the many battles that have been fought, and you must absolutely celebrate and rejoice in those. I am convinced those wins will serve as the ammunition and the grit needed should a new war be waged against either of us.

Lesson #18: Men must prepare to endure and even navigate these things emotionally if their wife or significant other suffers such a ruthless diagnosis. Yes, I am aware that breast cancer is not the death sentence it once was, now that we have such advancements in medical treatment, early detection, and even prevention methods. I am referring, however, to the survivor allowing cancer to serve as a catalyst of death to their relationships and marriages. This sentiment can seem a bit harsh, overstated, insensitive, and unnecessary; however, it does not alter what could be the reality for so many. I know

I am not alone, with 255,000 women and 2,300 men diagnosed with breast cancer annually. I am not sure how many married families are impacted, but it is worth saying that spouse to spouse is truly demanding.

As I ponder, I can also empathize with those not married but dating or pursuing meaningful, loving relationships. I can imagine how difficult it would be or the courage required to share your personal cancer journey with a stranger hoping they can accept it, appreciate your struggle, applaud your triumph, understand battles of low self-esteem or confidence, and recognize the beauty in your body's scars. To also want the man or significant other to appreciate and desire new and improved breasts- although not completely natural/real. You would hope that money is not an issue for the person they date because they will be asked to possibly consider inheriting medical debt. They may or may not be okay with the cost of high insurance premiums or no insurance at all. Will they ever accept that their time with you may be short-term? This sounds so horrible even as I write it, but we are all yet human regardless of the Christ in us. Not saying these things does not make them any less true. However, we all hope that decency wins out, that tolerance is common, and that love truly does conquer all. See, everyone cannot handle trial by fire. Surviving this kind of heat requires that you demonstrate courage and conviction while revealing critical vulnerabilities and

A Note

"Realizing that you both have battle scars when the smoke clears is a moment to look forward to because it symbolizes you survived together and it made you stronger, fortifying your union."

humbly seeking support. It challenges your faith in untold ways. It tests the strength and foundation that supports the willingness to sacrifice all. Teresa L. Mackey, my wife, is a testament to the characteristics and traits a survivor must have to endure cancer and life's most difficult battles it causes. I get to see it and experience all that she is daily. We both draw energy and inspiration from this journey and the battle we have fought.

Since entering remission, we like to think we are better and stronger for it. We support breast cancer advocacy and funding. We participate in breast cancer walks for healthy living and support and are reminded of the journey of those who had to walk the same path and are still here sharing encouragement and inspiration. They remind us of the courage gained and required to maintain those positive vibes. My wife practices yoga with a support group, which is completely out of her comfort zone. We both have met a host of new acquaintances and even made some new friends along the way. We now know who actually gives a damn in our circle. Most importantly, from the countless doctors, nurses, staff, colleagues, employers, and a complete list of strangers, the battles and scars have shown us the beauty in life and the people in it. I know that it can always get worse, so we choose to rejoice in every individual win because they will lead to a great victory.

We learned so much during this journey. We learned that people's character is so much greater than the color of their skin. Nurses, doctors, healthcare workers, and breast cancer survivors of all different gender and races kneel at your bedside, make calls, send happies, and provide encouragement. Most importantly, they are willing to offer prayer on your behalf at any given moment. I do not know about you, but I think that's the stuff the world needs more of. We experienced it firsthand, so we know these sentiments exist. You move forward with hope in humanity, desiring the same support, respect, and love shown to the cancer community that can extend to the masses. My wife and I are stronger, and I am a better husband, father, and person because of our battles and victory.

My wife, early on, wanted to maintain privacy throughout the cancer journey. What I quickly discovered, and I believe she did too, is that you absolutely must identify your fight champions. There were times when my wife experienced loneliness, felt I was sometimes insensitive, needed to talk to someone with a bit more understanding, or quite possibly she did not even know what she needed. This is why it is essential to have a group of people to whom she can confide her true feelings. It was equally important that I had a support system to do the same when approaching my wit's end. Friends, family, and acquaintances <u>are not a luxury – but a necessity</u>. Read that again.

Having an outlet to allow me to continue some sense of normalcy and peace was a saving grace of sorts. These brief, mandatory, or extended activities will allow you to be your very best. For me, it was golf, my motorcycle (which I chose not to tell her on occasions), and cooking. Find your outlet or resource which will allow you to be your very best you. It is worth noting that it could create resentment, frustration, and stress if done in excess. You must identify the sweet spot and balance between one's personal rejuvenation and what could appear to be avoidance of her which could cause feelings of loneliness or neglect. Remember, you are the protector and provider. This includes providing an environment for mature, transparent sharing of feelings where you and your spouse can feel safe without the threat of repercussion.

Faith is taking the first step even when you don't see the whole staircase. ~Martin Luther King, Jr.

Chapter 14

FAITH
I'm A Believer!

When waging war against an enemy as persistent and deadly as cancer, you have to lean on God, religion, and faith. Or do you? The first cry is, "Why me, why us?" You start to review and compare your moral and faithful calendar of life; and know in your heart that as a faithful servant, you deserve better. However, in the end, the very implication of asking "why me?" implies that it is best for someone else to carry the burden, pass the test, run the race, or any cliché you wish to use. The question creates doubt, which tests our faith. In case you were wondering, I am way over my head discussing religious matters; however, it is inescapable when discussing life's unexpected trials and tragedies, especially when one needs courage and strength to persevere.

My wife is a practicing Catholic, and I am Baptist. One of the core principles of our belief system is faith. God, religion, and faith may seem ancillary to some due to doctors, science, and medicine; however, it is critical for us. I find strength in God's words; Trust in the Lord with all your heart, and do not lean on your own understanding; I can do all things through Christ who strengthens me; for we live by faith, not by sight; and one of my favorite scriptures regarding faith and healing states, everything is possible for one who believes. However, it is easy to become cynical and weak because your body and mind desire convenient answers to your prayers. Why allow the negativity of the world to persist? Why do the good continue to die young? Why unleash a disease like cancer on your people that kills and destroys them, oh Powerful One? Yes, you question everything; Is the Bible just another book? Is faith as absent and artificial as hope, and does religion equate to my connection and passion for cooking? Yes, everything is questioned. We learned that it was not

> **A Note**
> "Faith is only strengthened by times of testing. It's like a muscle, if you don't exercise it, you will lose it."

about convenience but about faith and victory in His time. Needless to say, my faith was tested. Only my wife can truly speak to the depth of her own faith, and I will leave it to her to one day do so. As for now, we claim victory and accept God's will; and give Him all the honor and glory. Let the church say AMEN!

Accentuate the positive, eliminate the negative,

and latch onto the affirmative. ~Bing Crosby

Chapter 15

THE POSITIVES
Focus, Track, and Cherish

I have spoken about this throughout the book, but I felt it needed a chapter of its own, as it will prove to be one of your greatest weapons. This chapter may also be the hardest to digest simply because the subject forces you to daily identify the most elusive elements of life, often hiding in plain sight- the positives. In fact, hearing someone say, "Find the silver lining!" in a place where you may feel completely lost yourself could incite searing rage at times. "What do you mean, silver lining?" "That's completely ridiculous!" However, I find encouragement in another of my favorite scriptures, Philippians 4:8, which says:

Finally, brethren, whatsoever things are true, whatsoever things are honest, whatsoever things are just, whatsoever things are pure, whatsoever things are lovely, whatsoever things are of good report; if there be any virtue, and if there be any praise, think on these things.

It teaches us to focus on the positive. It's not saying ignore bad situations, but balance your thought life so that you can still function. Your wife depends on it. Your children depend on it. Believe it or not, YOU depend on it. So, whether you are just starting this journey, in the middle, or at the end, if you have any hope of surviving and thriving past it, you must take control of your headspace. **Lesson #19:** Don't let fear or negative thoughts overwhelm you! Realistically, you will have good, bad, and some really bad days, but make it a priority to start each day with something positive. When possible, include your spouse, giving them positive affirmations, long comforting hugs, and soft passionate kisses. Another technique would be to think of three different things you are grateful for every day. I know this seems like nothing, but consider you are carrying a new heavy load. That means you will have to venture into new territory and learn new survival techniques so that you can be the support your wife desperately needs.

Speaking of my wife, and I should have done this earlier, but I am sure you have noticed by now that I am writing this book in a past, present, and future voice. Can I just brag on my wife a bit? Dr. Teresa L. Mackey has over 22 years of combined teaching and administrative experience in higher education. Her passion is truly in the classroom, where she teaches College Algebra, Calculus, and Trigonometry. I still do not quite understand how and why anyone would want to teach math. She is one of the most intellectual and thoughtful people I know. As the oldest sibling of 6, she is always in assist, survivor, and *mother-protector* mode.

Teresa loves and adores her family. She can be a bit feisty, but I respect that- especially when others have offended or insulted her. We made a commitment from the very beginning not to curse or disrespect the other; however, I have heard her string together a list of curse words that would make Samuel Jackson proud. She has been through the storm and came out the other side stronger, more committed, and more spirited than ever before. Teresa is my partner in crime, and we both play our roles for the mutual benefit of our family and friends. She is a survivor.

A Note

"It is of a truth that half the battle is in your mind, so it is imperative that you condition your mind with positive thoughts."

These are the positive things I chose to focus on and remind myself of every day. In my eyes, my wife was already a hero... a rock star... a soldier...a beauty queen... my good thang. Yes, I said thang. This way, you know I really meant it!

I referenced earlier that my wife journals diligently. I think it is also a good idea for husbands to journal their experiences. Sometimes life comes at you so fast that you cannot actually be in the moment or process what is happening. A journal allows you to reflect, release, and resolve. "Atta-boys", "good jobs", and other affirmations, whatever you want to call them... need to be given; and ladies, please do know it is nice to return the sentiment!

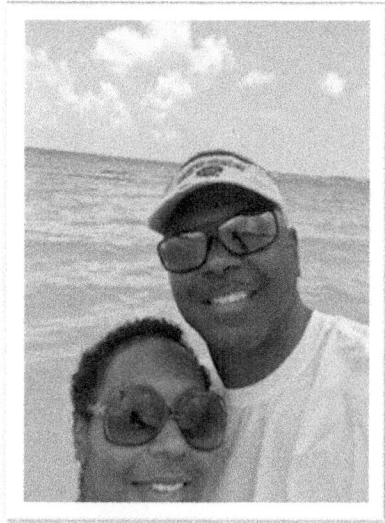

Rise when you think you can't, crawl if you can't walk, and try even if you think you'll fail. Life is short so make it count. ~Genny Small

Chapter 16

LESSONS LEARNED
Mission Possible

Benjamin Franklin once said, "If you fail to plan, you are planning to fail!" **Lesson #20:** Men, write this across your forehead. Trust me; it is priceless wisdom, a gift that keeps on giving while navigating your own path. The most significant part of your success strategy is a well-thought-out plan for good communication, organization of the house, unexpected sickness, childcare, and your relationship. Go with me here for a moment. Some will get anxiety just reading this because they like spontaneity and may feel boxed in or controlled by a plan. That is not the case. I want you to see the value in rehearsing certain things in your mind before it plays out in real-time. You respond differently, and you receive differently. Did you hear that? Reread it. This one act can keep your stress level low, open communication lines, and make you both very happy. You know the saying, "Happy wife, happy life!" Where's the lie?

I hope in some small way I have helped you or at least stirred in you the resolve to know that you are not alone and there is help available to you. I do not have all the answers, and we are still learning more every day about the formidable adversary called cancer. As you can see from my story, there are probably many people around you that are happy and eager to answer questions and encourage you and your wife. Do not be afraid to ask for help or be too ashamed to say how you feel. Can I be honest? I believe not getting assistance or bottling up these new and unfamiliar feelings is the perfect recipe for another big storm in your relationship; a storm called Resentment & Bitterness. Remember, to

> **A Note**
> "You can't take someone somewhere you've never been. You can't help someone until you first realize you need help as well."

have victory in this war, you and your spouse must be united against your common enemy. Mistakenly believing that you can handle it properly in all your masculine pride, without assistance, will ensure you both die on the battlefield, be it emotionally, spiritually, or.... physically.

That being said, the focus of this book has been primarily on my processes, reactions, interpretations, and the support system for my wife's battle with cancer. It was written to be a resource for men who find themselves in a similar position because, candidly, there was no guidance to assist me; at least, nothing I felt would add value. You know, like a book on "How to care for your wife, speak cancer terminology, respect her privacy, communicate, and express feelings of unconditional love for dummies." I truly believe this book can serve as a resource for many that may find themselves in a similar position.

Most importantly, I would encourage wives or female counterparts to sincerely explore this book to better understand the experiences from their husbands' perspectives and through my firsthand accounts, learn to evaluate and examine their own attitudes, behaviors, and responses. Even though you may be facing your most difficult personal challenge, it will help you empathize with the new, unfamiliar role your husband is forced to embrace. You both must learn to communicate with purpose, trust, and support each other's deficiencies as he learns to function as both primary care provider and devoted husband. Acknowledging this change in role will be important and pay dividends as it relates to their commitment, enthusiasm, and happiness.

Lastly, and this is an assumption on my part, but I believe this book and these principles can help anyone regardless of the type of cancer. There is an old saying, "Pressure can either burst pipes or make diamonds."

Engaging in a cancer battle can bring about both reactions on the same day. However, I offer these nuggets of wisdom to help produce more diamonds. Many are worth repeating from the text, and others, while not specifically addressed in the text, will contribute to a successful path to victory- remission.

Men

1.   Be there, be physically and mentally present always. Your absence will be personally noted, not only by your wife but also by your circle of family, friends, and supporters.

2.   Develop relationships with the doctors, nurses, and staff. This indicates that you are engaged and fully invested.

3.   Give your wife space and time to grieve the diagnosis before you hop into fix-it mode. It is important that she accepts the reality and establishes her attitude for the journey.

4.   Research, research, research. Learn and gain an understanding of all things breast cancer. It will help with communication, providing medical care, and demonstrates commitment.

5. Do NOT miss treatments. Treatment can be one of the loneliest and most vulnerable activities.

6. Understand the side effects of treatment and surgery. The side effects are harsh and proper planning can help neutralize some of the discomfort and pain. Be prepared to ensure proper remedies are available and ready.

7. Do the small things big, and the big things exceptionally. What you consider to be a trivial request or task is meaningful and adds value.

8. Understand that intimacy may be less frequent, if at all, but has nothing to do with you. Place the blame where it belongs, on the cancer and not your wife.

9. Compliment her appearance. Be genuine and do so frequently. The compliments will help revitalize her confidence and give reassurance of your attraction to her.

10. Open your mouth and tell her you LOVE her. I've touched on this a bit already but remember the *love*. It may seem a bit *weak* because you are a man, but let's be clear, this is your WIFE. She is part of you, mother to your children, your partner in unspecified life crimes, and the yin to your yang. Reflecting on why you fell in love with this woman and seeing her now as the woman she is becoming can only enhance what you already have. Trust me. There is nothing more attractive than a woman's strength, courage, and determination.

11.   Communicate! There are two types of communication: effective and ineffective. Whether we admit it or not, most of us are communicating ineffectively. Even those that think they communicate well! Communicating means listening, not just giving your input. Communication can be verbal or nonverbal. Take time to learn your wife's love language. Thank me later.

12.   Make time for good distractions. Plan meaningful activities to help eliminate the constant thoughts and focus on cancer.

13.   Do not forget the value of hugs and kisses. They create comfort and demonstrate reassurance.

14.   Do not frown upon counseling/therapy. It can create awareness and offer solutions.

15.   Rely on your network and circle of friends. These people will be present when you cannot be, they will allow her to speak her truth when she cannot be with you, and they provide additional resources.

16.   Make weekly alone time a priority. You need to have outlets to reduce stress and hit the reset button. This principle was unique for us because we had the added disadvantage of being quarantined for several months due to Covid. You need alone time to yourself. This does not make you selfish. This keeps you sane. Golf, go to the gym, go running, go shopping, paint, take a cooking class, and do something by yourself to maintain balance in your life.

17. Laugh a little or a lot, but by any means necessary, laugh.

18. Understand that her body will change, and your perception matters. New breasts are weapons and can and will be used against you.

Women

1. While it is ultimately the female's body, attempting to make decisions regarding treatment and surgery together will demonstrate partnership and cultivate a sense of harmony immediately and determine the approach going forward.

2. Acknowledge the effort being demonstrated. A compliment and a "thank you" can pay big dividends.

3. Communicate your true feelings. Keeping them in will make you angry, bitter, and resentful. It will help avoid and resolve conflicts.

4. Summon the energy and desire to engage in some form of intimacy. Understand that your husband needs your touch- not just wants it - **NEEDS**!

5. It is ok to acknowledge that you like your new breasts, even if they may no longer provide stimulation. Inform your spouse of this fact.

6. Your attitude will impact all things. Do your very best always to remain positive—good vibes are easier to vibe to.

Here is one last nugget that applies to both husbands and wives. DO NOT deny what you feel. Allow yourself to feel what you feel! Do not invalidate what you feel because it seems inappropriate, harsh, or even selfish. You cannot possibly hope to heal or adequately process what you will not acknowledge. So, if you feel angry, be angry, but do not let anger control you. Do not allow it to override your ability to think rationally. Do not allow it to forge words out of your mouth like a renegade rocket. Take a moment to calm yourself down. Try to remove yourself from the situation before saying something you can't take back. Track what set the anger off. Get to the root, the true cause of how you are feeling in that moment. Then process it. How can you handle it better? Am I angry because I feel I have no control over the situation? Do I feel like I am not being heard or that my feelings don't matter?

A Note
"It's been said, "There are no losses, only lessons. The fact that some would disagree says how crucial the right perspective is."

Once you identify the root, then you can strategize how to change your response. The worst thing you can do is bottle up your feelings and push them down like they do not exist. Have you ever seen the top blow off of a pressure cooker? Yep! That's you without correctly processing your emotions. We are not robots, and when we internalize things for too long, we become bitter, resentful, or lash out at the wrong time. As a result, we often shut down the possibility of effective communication. Again, feel what you feel. Acknowledge it. Process it. Channel it.

I must admit that I went back and forth in the early stages, trying to determine if writing this book was a good idea. I believed in the purpose, but I had doubts, lots of doubts. I knew it would be extremely personal, quite revealing, uncomfortable, and embarrassing on a number of levels. This would be true for both my wife and me. I was near completion of the book before I sat down with my wife to share the book project and obtain her buy-in and support. I wanted and needed her undeniable approval. I told her that she could eliminate any stories, details, pictures, or text she felt was too sensitive or a bridge too far stretched. I had one stipulation; she could not alter the text that established how I felt in the moment because I needed the feelings to be real and authentic for the reader. This approach gave me the courage to continue writing; however, my plan was only to allow my wife to review the final draft. I felt that if she reviewed the book in full context and saw our story come to life, she may be less inclined to suggest numerous deletions.

I would ultimately receive her endorsement with very few edits. She was willing to own her public discomfort, demonstrating again what a remarkable lady she is.

More than ever, I now recognize the value my wife finds in chronicling her cancer journey in her journal. Writing this book has been one of the most therapeutic activities I have engaged in. It has allowed me to express openly how I felt regarding the battles, processes, attitudes, communication, and behaviors. It presented another voice to speak to my wife. This format, I believe, has allowed her to view my internal struggles differently; gain a greater understanding of my sacrifice, and acknowledge the depth of my role in her recovery. I suspect it has opened up the door for even more meaningful, transparent dialogue, which can be difficult. I view this level of communication and comprehension as critical and a definite benefit of our cancer battle.

As I write this text and ponder each battle, it is at this moment that I realize the answers to the questions were less about me and more about the circumstances that had brought us to this very point, cancer. We would both be forced to grow if we were to claim victory. This was true from each battle fought and won, and not just victory over cancer but victory over our marriage. Almost unbeatable trials and tribulations were frequent visitors in our household. Neither should be underestimated as it relates to cancer. However, collectively, we faced our individual fears, learned tolerance, and identified new and unfamiliar ways to express our unconditional love for each other. These principles would sustain us, provide direction, and yield power for whatever is to come.

I personally learned that I could be loving, caring, and patient; however, it was sometimes overshadowed by temporary moments of insensitivity, frustration, and selfishness. Yes, I wanted to continue doing those things that I had grown accustomed to; but I had to learn to accept that sacrifice was necessary and required. So, I did. I did a lot, but most importantly, I am committed to doing it all again and again and again, if necessary.

I believe your purpose can sometimes be temporary and situational. You must recognize the moment and thrive in it. I believe you can always choose goodness and respect. Those two can define who you are in any battle and determine who you are in your marriage or relationship. I believe sacrifice comes with its own reward. No one knows what tomorrow may offer, whether it is a new battle or reward. This is my testimony, and maybe someday, we will have an opportunity to read hers. Fortunately, I have received my reward in knowing that my wife is healthy, cancer-free, and living her best life on her own terms. I pray the same reward for each of you.

"Victory is always possible for the person who refuses to stop fighting." ~ Napoleon Hill.

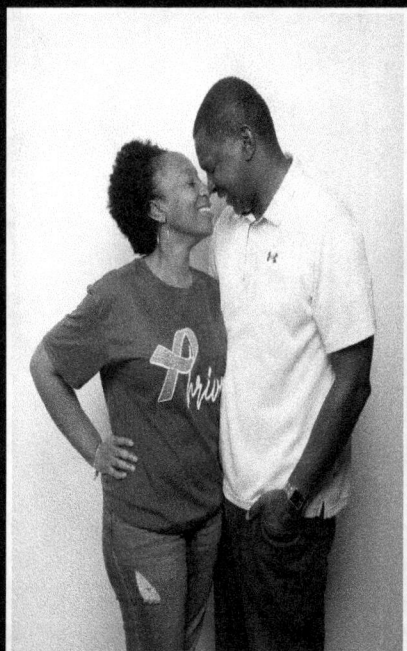 

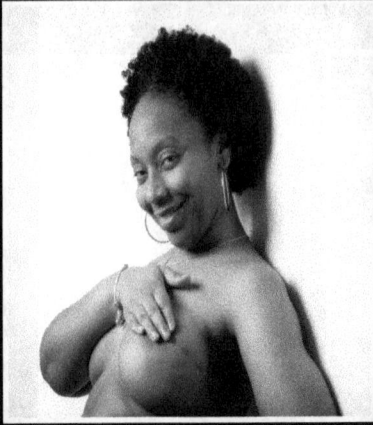

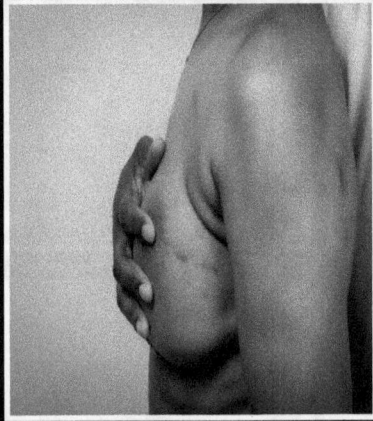

Dr. Shawn Mackey, Sr., was born and raised in Silver Creek, Mississippi, where he learned early in life that hard work and perseverance have their rewards. During the summer months, Dr. Mackey used to work as a truck loader for his uncle's pulpwood business. The days were hot, the hours were long, and the work was grueling. This work inspired Dr. Mackey to seek better opportunities for himself and his family. He quickly realized that education and knowledge would serve as a catalyst for a pathway to achieving success in life. After graduating from high school, Dr. Mackey attended Delta State University. He takes great pride in being a three-time graduate of Delta State University (go Fighting Okra) with a Bachelor of Science Degree in Criminal Justice (1997), a Bachelor of Arts in Psychology (1997), and a Master's Degree in Social Science Education (2000). Dr. Mackey continued to prepare for the future he envisioned for himself by obtaining his Doctor of Education Degree from the University of Memphis in the area of Higher Education Administration (2008).

Dr. Mackey is a champion for education both personally and professionally and has worked in higher education for over twenty years, serving as a senior team member at the Mississippi Community College Board for the last fifteen. In his current role as Deputy Executive Director of Accountability at the Mississippi Community College Board (MCCB), he supervises Athletics, Research and Effectiveness, Monitoring, and Resource Development for Mississippi's fifteen community colleges. He is also intricately involved in Academic and Student Affairs, Workforce, Career and Technical Education, and Curriculum Development. He is committed to instituting real educational change regarding student access, instruction, and resources. He diligently works to level the playing field for all students. Dr. Mackey wholeheartedly subscribes to Nelson Mandela's belief that "education is the most powerful weapon by which to change the world" as he believes that education fosters tolerance, promotes self-sufficiency and self-confidence, and encourages students to maximize their individual potential.

One of Dr. Mackey's proudest professional achievements was completing the Mississippi Community College Leadership Academy (MCCLA) in 2009 and traveling to the United Kingdom to study and evaluate the community college system in London and Wales.

Dr. Mackey is an entrepreneur and the founder of SCM Consulting & Investments, LLC, a property renovation and management company, and a proud member of Alpha Phi Alpha Fraternity. He enjoys traveling the world, golfing, riding motorcycles, and competition barbecue cooking. He believes in the power of faith, family, love, and laughter. Above all, he takes the greatest pride in being the husband of Dr. Teresa L. Mackey and the father of three boys: Christopher, Shawn, Jr., and Matthew.

Learn more about Dr. Shawn C. Mackey by visiting
www.shawncmackey.com.

SCAN ME

www.ingramcontent.com/pod-product-compliance
Lightning Source LLC
Chambersburg PA
CBHW072003090426
42740CB00011B/2073